PRAISE FOR
ANTHONY DE MELLO

✦

"Anthony De Mello's new book is like a coaching manual for life.
Our feelings create our internal chemistry, which can be life-enhancing or
self-destructive depending upon our feelings and thoughts.
De Mello's book and wisdom can help you to heal and survive.
I know from my experience as a physician what it can do for you.
So read it and become an all-star performer."
—**Bernie Siegel, MD**, author of *Love, Medicine & Miracle*
and *No Endings Only Beginnings*

"In *A Year with Anthony De Mello*, readers will once again be inspired by
his incredibly powerful teachings and insights. De Mello carves a path
for us to move forward in peace and happiness in this new,
practical workbook."
—**C. James Jensen**, author of
Expand the Power of Your Subconscious Mind

"*A Year with Anthony De Mello* takes you on a journey of spiritual awakening through 52 simple, yet deep stories followed by self-observation
prompts. The stories open the heart; the reflections re-program the mind.
Read this book carefully, do the practices, and you will discover within
yourself a natural state of peace, love, and happiness."
—**Nayaswami Kamala**, publisher of *Spiritual Life Magazine*

Waking Up Week by Week

A Year with
Anthony
De Mello

Anthony De Mello

Edited by Don Joseph Goewey

BEYOND WORDS
Portland, Oregon

This book is dedicated to the memory of

James Desmond Towey (1937-2022)

who, for nearly three decades, was key in seeing that the transformative work of Anthony De Mello was kept alive and available to the world.

BEYOND WORDS

1750 S.W. Skyline Blvd, Suite 20
Portland, Oregon 97221-2543
503-531-8700 / 503-531-8773 fax
www.beyondword.com

First Beyond Words hardcover edition December 2022

BEYOND WORDS PUBLISHING is an imprint of Simon & Schuster, Inc., and the Beyond Words logo is a registered trademark of Beyond Words Publishing, Inc.

For information about special discounts for bulk purchases, please contact Beyond Words Special Sales at 503-531-8700 or specialsales@beyondword.com.

Managing editor: Lindsay S. Easterbrooks-Brown
Editor: Don Joseph Goewey
Copyeditor: Madison Schultz
Proofreader: Ashley Van Winkle
Design: Devon Smith
Composition: William H. Brunson Typography Services

Manufactured in the United States of America

10 9 8 7 6 5 4 3 2 1

Library of Congress Control Number: 2022936216

ISBN 978-1-58270-869-0
ISBN 978-1-58270-871-3 (ebook)

The corporate mission of Beyond Words Publishing, Inc.: *Inspire to Integrity*

CONTENTS

PART 1: THE KINGDOM OF JOY

PART 2: THE LAND OF LOVE

CONTENTS

PART 3: REDISCOVERING LIFE

PART 4: THE ME, THE I, AND GOD

PART 5: FAITH

PART 6: ONE LAST WORD—ALL IS WELL

FOREWORD

Awarm welcome to this workbook by Father Anthony De Mello. Let me offer a few suggestions that may help even before you start.

First, skimming or speed-reading does not help in anything written by Tony De Mello. You don't want to miss the mysteries and challenges waiting for you. I can assure you that a patient reading will bring some rich rewards.

Second, and just as important as the first, prepare for surprises. If you don't encounter any, better to go back and read that paragraph or chapter again. At times, the familiar contains the surprise. At other times, it will be something far from customary or something that's even disturbing. Tony's stories are chosen not only for their entertainment value but because, in Tony's own words, "a story is the shortest distance between a human being and the truth." Children always want to hear a story more than just once. And some adults feel the same way. That could explain why our Lord's stories like the prodigal son or the good shepherd, for example, are so precious to us millennia after he uttered them. And Tony makes no apologies for stories from different cultures and different countries. They have much to tell us about our human nature.

That's no surprise. What may come as a surprise is Tony's warning about accepting or rejecting his statements. It is really part of the work when dealing with this workbook. Here is Tony's admonition: you must not accept my words out of respect but should analyze them the way the Buddha advised seekers, "the way the goldsmith analyzes gold—by cutting, scraping, rubbing, melting." That is the attitude Tony wished the reader to have when evaluating anything he wrote. For him, the argument from authority will not be used. To require such high standards from his readers might qualify in itself as a surprise.

One final question may be occurring to you as you start reading—or should I say working through—this book: Will it be worth my effort? Am I really going to be free from what seems like a program of endless self-improvement? Or is this just the same old search that leads me nowhere? Good question! And one impossible to answer with promises or guarantees. My own experience, for example, is no guarantee of what your experience or anyone else's might be. Even two similar people might respond differently to Tony's suggestions and challenges. So there is no absolutely guaranteed, predictable outcome that can be offered for everyone investing their time and effort.

But it's not a foolish gamble, I can assure you.

Quite apart from my own years of friendship with Tony at Fordham University, prior to his death on June 2, 1987, I have also had the privilege to hear from many people their personal estimate of how their lives have been affected by Tony's books, conferences, retreats, friendship. They always all seem to contain one central idea: He changed my life! No matter their age, background, religion or lack thereof, Tony had a way of impacting people. That could be a coincidence or an unrepeatable happenstance, but I don't think so.

A few weeks ago, the De Mello Center received a request that caught my eye. It was from a publisher asking to be allowed to print Tony's books in several new languages and countries not yet having them available to the public. The request reflects a great deal of diversity among Tony's readers. So it could be that more than three decades after his death, Tony's wisdom still speaks authentically about spirituality today. I believe you will find this out for yourselves in the pages of this workbook. Of course, none of this gives a final, definitive answer to your question about the value of reading the book and doing the work. There are too many variables involved. But if the suggestions and examples that I have offered allow you to confidently turn the pages of this book and continue reading it, I am relieved. And if your efforts at some future point result in your noticing a deeper sense of joy and peace within yourself and with others, I will not be at all surprised. That is simply the way Tony continues to do his work so well.

—Leo Daly, SJ,
trustee of the De Mello Spirituality Center

INTRODUCTION

Your task is not to seek for love, but merely to seek and find all of the barriers within yourself that you have built against it.

—A Course in Miracles

HOW TO USE THIS BOOK

This book invites you on a spiritual retreat with Anthony (Tony) De Mello. Although Tony was a Jesuit priest, this book is not a Catholic book or even a Christian book. It is a spiritually centered book. As Tony often said, "Spirituality is about waking up." Thus, this book offers you a practical spiritual approach to what people everywhere are searching for and rarely find. Namely, the fountainhead of peace and joy that hides in every human heart. The best way to introduce you to the book is to use the words Tony used to open the first day of the retreats he conducted when he still walked with us. Here's what Tony said to participants:

> People are asleep. They're living on delusions, on crazy ideas about everything, about love, about relationships, about happiness, about joy, about what the world should be, who they should be, and what they should want. Spirituality is about waking up. In facilitating awakening, I will be moving from one thing to another and returning to themes again and again, because that's the way to really grasp what I'm saying. I've got different themes—love, awakening, freedom, happiness, call it what you wish—but they are all about the same thing. If it doesn't hit you the first time, it might the second time, and what doesn't hit one person might hit another.

What is extremely important, if you want to wake up, is to go in for what I call Self-Observation. Be aware of what you're saying, be aware of what you're feeling, be aware of what you're thinking, be aware of how you're acting. Be aware of where you're coming from, what your motives are, but with no judgment, no attitude, no interference, no attempt to change, only to understand, for you only change what you understand. What you do not understand and are not aware of, you repress. But when you understand it, it changes. Awareness releases reality to change you, but you've got to see that for yourself. The moment you see that a belief is false, you're free. As you begin to move ahead on this path, you'll discover this for yourself. Don't expect that somehow I am going to do it for you. That's another delusion, that someone else can liberate you. Not even the greatest guru can take a single step for you. It is you who must become aware of the illusions that have been programmed into you that block the truth. I can promise you this: I have not known a single person who gave time to being aware who didn't see a difference in a matter of weeks. The quality of your life changes, so you don't have to take it on faith anymore. You see it; you're different. You react differently. In fact, you react less and act more. You see things you've never seen before. You're much more energetic, much more alive. People think that if they had no cravings, they'd be like deadwood. But in fact they'd lose their tension. Get rid of your fear of failure, your tensions about succeeding, you will be yourself. Relaxed. When your illusions crumble, you will look out at the world and say, "My, how different everything looks."

TONY'S WORKSHOP IN A BOOK

This book was designed to offer you daily encounters with Tony De Mello, week by week, over the course of a year. As such, the book is divided into fifty-two segments or chapters, with each week's segment presenting a key passage from one of Tony De Mello's masterworks. I strongly suggest you read the stories in the order in which they are set down. The order imparts a teaching and a spirit that might be lost if the book is read haphazardly. Revisit the material each day throughout the week, digesting its themes and seeing how it relates to your life. Of course, you are free to engage this book in whatever way and at whatever pace suits you. If you want to take this course a day at a time or intermittently, you certainly are free to do so. But take it up and stay with it. If you do, you'll make the biggest discovery of your life.

THE PRACTICE

Following the passage for each week is a practice section called *Self-Observation*. In the Self-Observation section, Tony invites you to reflect on the current passage and engage with it directly and deeply to understand for yourself the way you have been programmed to see something that is not there—meaning the nightmare caused by the attachments, addictions, and illusion—and not see what is there, meaning the divinity all around you and within you that, if grasped, would transform your life into something meaningful and beautiful and rich.

Each Self-Observation section is prefaced with a story that relates to the preceding passage for the week. The stories are from one of Anthony De Mello's books of spiritual stories. Here is how to engage with these stories: Read the story twice at first. On the first reading, you might be amused by the tale. On the second reading, take it deeper. Reflect on it. Apply it to your life. Then read the story a third time after you have reflected on it. Create a silence within yourself and let the story reveal to you its inner depth and meaning that goes beyond words and reflections. This will give you a feel for the mystical. You can journal in the empty pages that follow each Self-Observation section, but it may be that you need more writing space to capture what you wish to journal. In that case, purchase a spiral or bound notebook to use in tandem with this book.

Also, in the book's conclusion there is list of links to free resources that the De Mello Spirituality Center—the official archive of Anthony De Mello's work—makes available to you. These include the Anthony De Mello website, the De Mello app, and the social media and community platform centered on De Mello's approach to enlightenment.

It is my hope and the hope of the trustees of the De Mello Spirituality Center that through this book your heart will attain a great clarity.

—Don Joseph Goewey,
executive director of the De Mello Spirituality Center

PART 1

THE
KINGDOM
OF JOY

How sad, if you would have passed through life and never seen it
again with the eyes of a child. We need to return to paradise again;
we need to be redeemed again. We need to put off the old man,
the old nature, the conditioned self, and return to the state of
the child, but without being children.

—Anthony De Mello

WEEK 1

I discovered something not that long ago and it turned my life upside down. It revolutionized my life. I became a new man. This is what I'm going to share with you, although you might be thinking, "He's a priest, isn't he? How come he discovered this so late? Hadn't he read the Gospels?"

Of course I'd read the Gospels, but I hadn't seen it. It was right there, but I hadn't seen it. Later, having discovered it, I found it in all the major religious writings, and I was amazed. I mean, I was reading it, but I hadn't recognized it. I wished to God I'd found this when I was younger. Oh, what a difference it would have made.

So, how long will it take to give it to you? I'll be honest with you: I don't think it would take more than two minutes. Grasping it might take you twenty years, fifteen years, ten years, fifty-two weeks, one week, one day, ten minutes—who knows. You could read one chapter in this book and get it. It all depends on you.

Is it difficult to understand? It's so simple that a seven-year-old child could understand it. Isn't that amazing? Even now, as I think of it, I wonder, *Why didn't I see it?* I don't know why I didn't see it, but I didn't. Now, maybe you might see it today, or you might see part of it. What would you need to see it?

Just one thing: the ability to listen. That's all. Are you able to listen? If you can, you might get it.

Now, listening is not as easy as you might think. Why? Because we're always listening from fixed concepts, fixed positions, fixed prejudices. The kind of listening I am referring to means being alert. So, as you read this book and reflect on it, be alert. Be watchful. Hold the intention to listen with a fresh mind, without prejudices, without judging, without fixed formulas.

Listening, however, does not mean swallowing. That's gullibility. Don't take me or this book on faith. What I want you to do is to question everything I'm communicating, think about it, question it. Getting it doesn't mean agreeing with me. You could disagree with me and get it. Recall those lovely words of Buddha when he said, "Monks and scholars must not accept my words out of respect but must analyze them the way a goldsmith analyzes gold—by cutting, scraping, rubbing, melting." You have got to challenge everything, but challenge it from an attitude of openness, not from an attitude of stubbornness, resistance, narrowness. Challenge it all and be open as you do. When you do that, you're listening. You've taken another major step toward awakening.

> Hold the intention to listen with a fresh mind, without prejudices, without judging, without fixed formulas.

Self-Observation

I used to be stone deaf. I would see people stand up and go through all kinds of gyrations. They called it dancing. It looked absurd to me—until one day I heard the music!

—From *The Song of the Bird*

THIS WEEK, FOCUS ON THE FOLLOWING:

* Think of ways you wish to use this book as a distant preparation for being born into another, wider world. Open your mind to what suggests itself to you. Journal about it.
* Each day this week, before stepping into your everyday routine, ask yourself, "What do I want to make of my existence here on earth?" Then bring it closer, asking, "How do I want to live my life today?" Think of how you will seek autonomy and freedom: the risks you shall dare to take, the discomforts you shall welcome, the changes you will be open to.

Notes to Myself: _____

_____

_____

_____

_____

_____

_____

_____

_____

_____

_____

_____

_____

_____

WEEK 2

*Your problem is . . . whether you're going to live [your life] trying to
look good and creating the illusion that you have power over people and
circumstances, or whether you are going to taste it, enjoy it, and find
out the truth about who you are.*

—Anne Lamott

St. Paul said, "Rejoice always. Rejoice in the Lord. Again I say it: rejoice."
Let's suppose you want to grasp that lovely way of being in the world. Let's
suppose you want to see it. What do you have to do? You must understand
two truths about yourself. Here's the first truth: *your life is in a mess.* Of
course you might not like to hear that. It might insult you, which only
proves it's true. Say to someone *your life is in a mess* and they are likely to
object with, "What do you mean? I'm doing pretty well. I have a career;
I have good family relations. I have friends; I'm in love with a good man
or woman. Everybody likes me." Here's the acid test. Ever get stressed?
Ever get upset by anything? Ever feel lonely? Any heartache? Are all your
relationships going well with everybody? Are you anxious for the future?
Any whiff of worry, anger, upset? Ever suffer inner conflict, outer conflict?
The likely response to this will be, "Aren't we supposed to get upset?" Want
a clean, clear, simple answer? Here it is: No! "You mean, not be upset by
anything?" That's right, you heard me. Not by anything! "Oh, please, go
away," they will say. "I don't want to hear any more of your nonsense."
We've been given a theory that says to be upset is to be human. It is not
so. When I say your life is in a mess I mean you're a victim of heartache,
at least occasionally. A victim of inner conflict. There's emptiness staring at
you. You're scared. "You mean, we're not supposed to be scared?" they will
say. "No, you're not." "Not about anything?" "No, not about anything."

Fearlessness exists but you don't know what it means. And the tragedy is you don't even think it's available. Yet, it's so easy to get, but since society told you it's not available, you never try to find it; it's right here in the Sermon on the Mount, but you won't see it because you've been taught that it's not available. Mystics tell people that life is extraordinary, life is delightful: "You could enjoy it," they say. "You wouldn't have a minute of tension, not one. No pressure. No anxiety. Would you want that?" the mystics ask. The usual response is: "Not possible. Never been done. Cannot be done." That's the condition of people everywhere. They don't hear it. They won't listen. It's why your life remains in a mess. Do you want to clean it up? It would take five minutes, depending on how ready you are. It's so simple and it's so deadly serious that people miss it. And you can have it. How? So, first thing: Admit that your life is in a mess.

> "Fearlessness exists but you don't know what it means. And the tragedy is you don't even think it's available."

Here is the second truth—this is a bit tougher—admit you do not want to get out of the mess. Talk to any experienced psychologist and he or she will confirm that. The last thing a client wants is a cure. They don't want to get cured; they want relief. They want a pill; they want a salve; they want a Band-Aid. Give me back my wife. Give me back my money. Confirm for me that I'm right and they're wrong. They don't want to wake up; they don't want happiness. They want their illusions. Want to test this on yourself? Suppose you could be blissfully happy, but you're not going to get that college degree, or that hoped-for position, or win over that person you're interested in, or be a success. Are you ready to barter your degree or your job? Are you ready to barter that girlfriend of yours, or that boyfriend, for happiness? You're not going to be a success, you're going to fail and everybody is going to call you a bum, but you'll be blissfully happy. Are you ready to barter the good opinion of people for bliss? Most people aren't ready to do that. I saw an ad in the newspaper once showing a girl holding on to a boy and under the picture was a caption that read, "I don't want to be happy. I want to be miserable with you."

Self-Observation

A monkey on a tree hurled a coconut at the head of a Sufi. The man picked it up, drank the milk, ate the flesh, and made a bowl from the shell.

From The Song of the Bird

THIS WEEK, FOCUS ON THE FOLLOWING:

* Catch some of the subtle ways in which you make your happiness depend on people, possessions, circumstances, and outcomes. Journal about it.
* Begin to question the belief that without money, power, success, approval, a good reputation, romance, friendship, spirituality, or even God, you cannot be happy. Journal about this too.

NOTES TO MYSELF: _____

_____

_____

_____

_____

_____

_____

_____

_____

_____

_____

_____

_____

WEEK 3

People don't want to get out of the mess. They don't want happiness; they want money, they want fame, they want power, they want approval, they want their comforts. They want the little things that society has falsely taught them are essential for happiness. Those are the things that are creating the mess. It's the source of conflicts, anxieties, tensions, despair, heartache. If you could get rid of your attachment to all that, what you would be left with is sheer, undiluted happiness. The truth is you have happiness already, but these things obstruct it. When the mind is unobstructed, the result is truth. And when the heart is unobstructed, the result is joy and love. You would see it all around you, even in the poverty and death that's everywhere.

I was once introduced to a rickshaw puller in Calcutta. It's an awful existence, one human being riding in a rickshaw while another human being pulls him. The life span of these drivers is only ten to twelve years once they begin pulling the rickshaw. The name of the rickshaw driver I met was Ramchandra. Ramchandra had tuberculosis. At that time an organized crime ring was engaging in an illegal activity involving exporting skeletons, and they preyed upon impoverished rickshaw drivers because of their short lifespans. They bought the man's skeleton while he was still alive, all for the equivalent of ten dollars. The moment one of these drivers died, the thugs would pounce on the body, take it away, and decompose the body through some awful process until they had a skeleton to sell on the black market. Ramchandra had a wife, children, and all the squalor, misery, and disease that comes with abject poverty, and he had sold his

15

skeleton to support his family. You'd never think to find happiness in this man's life, and yet, he was all right. Nothing seemed to faze him. Nothing seemed to upset him. So, I asked him, "Why aren't you upset?" "About what?" he said. "Your future, the future of your kids." He simply said that he was doing the best he could and the rest was in the hands of God. "But what about your sickness?" I asked. "That causes suffering, doesn't it?" "A bit," Ramchandra said, "but I have to take life as it comes." I never once saw him in a bad mood and as I came to know him I realized I was in the presence of a mystic. I realized I was in the presence of life. It was right there. He was alive. By comparison, I was dead.

"To live like a king or queen spiritually means you know no anxiety at all, no inner conflict, no tensions, no pressures, no upset, no heartache.

Remember those lovely words of Jesus? Look at the birds of the air. Look at the flowers of the field. They don't have a moment of anxiety for the future. Ramchandra's life embodied those words. He was like the birds of the air. He understood the loveliness and the beauty of this experience we call human existence. Though exceedingly poor, Ramchandra lived like a king. Yes, more money would've helped, but he didn't need it, not to live from his heart. To live like a king or queen spiritually means you know no anxiety at all, no inner conflict, no tensions, no pressures, no upset, no heartache. Until you can transcend these reactions, your life remains a mess.

Another time I met a priest in St. Louis who was attending to an AIDS patient who was on his deathbed. Six months before, the doctors had told this man that he had only six months to live, and now, as he approached his death, he said to the priest, "The last six months have been the happiest time of my whole misspent life. In fact, I had never been happy until these last six months. I discovered happiness." He said the moment the doctor gave him his prognosis, he dropped tension, pressure, anxiety, and hope, and fell not into despair, but into happiness. He'd come alive.

Here were two men, one dying of AIDS, the other dying from abject poverty, both reduced to nothing, yet who were fully alive. They had found the key to the kingdom.

Self-Observation

On a bitterly cold day a master and his disciples were huddled around a fire.

One of the disciples, echoing his master's teachings, said, "On a freezing day like this I know exactly what to do!"

"What?" asked the others.

"Keep warm! And if that isn't possible, I still know what to do."

"What?"

"Freeze."

Present Reality cannot really be rejected or accepted.

To run away from it is like running away from your feet.

To accept it is like kissing your lips.

All you need to do is see, understand, and be at rest.

From *The Prayer of the Frog*

THIS WEEK, FOCUS ON THE FOLLOWING:

✴ Journal about someone in your life or someone you read or heard about who serves as inspiration for what it means to be fully alive; a person who, like Ramchandra or the gentleman in St. Louis dying of AIDS, transcended circumstances and found within themselves the key to the kingdom.

✳ To live like a king or queen spiritually means you know no anxiety at all, no inner conflict at all, no tensions, pressures, upset, or heartache. Until you can transcend these reactions, your life remains a mess. So, how is your life a mess? Journal about it.

Notes to Myself: _____

_____

_____

_____

_____

_____

_____

_____

_____

_____

_____

_____

_____

_____

_____

WEEK 4

One hears mystics speak of a divinity all around us that is within our grasp, a kingdom of joy that would make our lives meaningful and beautiful and rich, if we could only discover it. All mystics are unanimous on one thing: that all is well. Though everything is a mess, all is well. Strange paradox, to be sure. But, tragically, most people never get to see that all is well because they are asleep. They are having a nightmare. Reality is there; God is there. It's all there. But we're like the poor little fish in the ocean that says, "Excuse me, I'm looking for the ocean. Can you tell me where I can find it?" That's most of us. Pathetic, isn't it? If we would just open our eyes and see, then we would understand that all is well. But we're not seeing reality. It's like a stage magician who hypnotizes someone so that the person sees what is not there and does not see what is there.

> "All mystics are unanimous on one thing: that all is well. Though everything is a mess, all is well. Strange paradox, to be sure."

People have a vague idea as to what this divinity is, this Holiness, this Spirituality. They read books and consult gurus in an attempt to find out what they must do to gain this elusive thing. They pick up all sorts of methods, techniques, spiritual exercises, and formulas. Then, after years of fruitless striving, they become discouraged and confused and wonder

21

what went wrong. Most often, people blame themselves. They think, "If I'd only practiced those techniques more regularly, or if I had been more fervent or more generous, then I might have made it." But made what? They have no clear idea as to what the enlightenment that they seek is— but they certainly know that their lives are still unhappy. They still become anxious, insecure, and fearful; resentful and unforgiving; grasping, ambitious, and manipulative of people. They are still dissatisfied because they think they do not have enough money or power or success or fame or romance or virtue or spirituality. The source of their dissatisfaction is still greed and ambition, and its fruit is still restlessness and frustration. So, once again, they throw themselves with renewed vigor into what they think they need to do to fix themselves and attain their goal, and round and round they go.

Suppose there is a way of getting rid of all of that? Suppose there is a way to stop that tremendous drain of energy, health, and emotion that comes from such conflicts and confusion. Have you ever felt disgusted with life, sick at heart of constantly running away from fears and anxieties, weary of your begging rounds, exhausted from being dragged about helplessly by your attachments and addictions? When you have gone repeatedly around the cycle I just described, a time finally comes when you have had enough and want to call a halt to the whole process. The day you are discontented not because you want more of something but without knowing what it is you want, when you are sick at heart of everything that you have been pursuing so far and you are sick of the pursuit itself, then your heart will attain a great clarity, an insight that will cause you mysteriously to delight in everything and in nothing. The test that this discontent is divine is the fact that it has no trace of sadness or bitterness to it at all. On the contrary, even though it often arouses fear within your heart, it is always accompanied by joy, the joy of the kingdom.

Self-Observation

A man took his new hunting dog out on a trial hunt. Presently he shot a duck that fell into the lake. The dog walked over the water, picked the duck up, and brought it to his master.

The man was flabbergasted! He shot another duck. Once again, while he rubbed his eyes in disbelief, the dog walked over the water and retrieved the duck.

Hardly daring to believe what he had seen, he called his neighbor for a shoot the following day. Once again, each time he or his neighbor hit a bird the dog would walk over the water and bring the bird in. The man said nothing. Neither did his neighbor. Finally, unable to contain himself any longer, he blurted out, "Did you notice anything strange about that dog?"

The neighbor rubbed his chin pensively. "Yes," he finally said. "Come to think of it, I did! The son of a gun can't swim!"

It isn't as if life is not full of miracles. It's more than that: it is miraculous, and anyone who stops taking it for granted will see it at once.

From *The Prayer of the Frog*

THIS WEEK, FOCUS ON THE FOLLOWING:

* In your spiritual pursuit, what have you been seeking but not finding, glimpsing but not actualizing?
* What is the discontent you feel with your spiritual life? With your career? With your family life? Get in touch with the spark of discontent in your heart and journal about it.

Notes to Myself: _____

_____

_____

_____

_____

_____

_____

_____

_____

_____

_____

_____

_____

_____

WEEK 5

People often ask me, What do I need to do to change myself? If you are one of those people, I've got a big surprise for you! You don't have to do anything. In fact, the more you do, the worse it gets. That's why people are so weary. The trouble with people is that they're busy fixing things they don't even understand. It never strikes us that things don't need to be fixed. They really don't. This is a great illumination. Do you know what they need? They need to be *understood*. If they understood them, they'd change. How do you do that?

> It never strikes us that things don't need to be fixed. They really don't. This is a great illumination. . . . They need to be *understood*.

1. The first thing you will need to do is get in touch with all the negative feelings that you're not even aware of. Lots of people have negative feelings they're not aware of. Lots of people are depressed and they're not aware they are depressed. It's only when they make contact with joy that they fully understand how depressed they were. What negative feelings? Gloominess, for instance. You're feeling gloomy and moody. You feel self-hatred or guilt. You feel that life is pointless, that it makes no sense;

you've got hurt feelings, you're feeling nervous and tense. Get in touch with those feelings first.

2. The second step is to understand that the feeling is in you, not in reality. That's such a self-evident thing, but do you think people know it? So stop trying to change reality. Stop trying to change the other person. Watch! Observe! Watch everything in you and around you as far as possible and watch it as if it were happening to someone else. What does that last sentence mean? It means that you do not personalize what is happening to you. It implies that you look at things as if you have no connection with them whatsoever.

3. The third step: Never identify with that feeling. It has nothing to do with the "I." Don't define your essential self in terms of that feeling. Don't say, "I am depressed." If you want to say depression is there, that's fine; if you want to say gloominess is there, that's fine. But not: I am gloomy. You're defining yourself in terms of the feeling. That's your illusion; that's your mistake. There is a depression there right now, there are hurt feelings there right now, but let it be, leave it alone. It will pass. Everything passes, everything. Your depressions and your thrills have nothing to do with happiness. Those are the swings of the pendulum. If you seek kicks or thrills, get ready for depression. Do you want your drug? Get ready for the hangover. One end of the pendulum swings to the other.

4. The fourth step: Acknowledge how we always want someone else to change so that we will feel good. But has it ever struck you that even if your wife changes or your husband changes, what does that do to you? You're just as vulnerable as before; you're just as idiotic as before; you're just as asleep as before. You are the one who needs to change. You keep insisting, "I feel good because the world is

right." Wrong! The world is right because I feel good. If at first there is a sluggishness in practicing awareness, don't force yourself. That would be an effort again. Just be aware of your sluggishness without any judgment or condemnation. Step by step, let whatever happens happen. Real change will come when it is brought about—not by your ego, but by reality. Awareness releases reality to change you.

Self-Observation

"What must I do for Enlightenment?"

"Nothing."

"Why not?"

"Because Enlightenment doesn't come from doing—it happens."

"Then can it never be attained?"

"Oh yes it can."

"How?"

"Through nondoing."

"And what does one do to attain nondoing?"

"What does one *do* to go to sleep or to wake up?"

From *One Minute Wisdom*

THIS WEEK, FOCUS ON THE FOLLOWING:

✳ Carefully review the simple steps to becoming aware. Read this chapter each week for the next three weeks to master these steps. Commit to using these steps throughout the day, integrating them into your way of being, your way of consciously relating to what happens in you and around you each day throughout the day. At the end of the day, you can use the aid below to track how often this week you stepped back from your reactions, using these steps to become more objectively aware of thoughts and emotions as they happen in you.

Tracking How Consciously Aware You Are Becoming

Frequency	Day 1	Day 2	Day 3	Day 4	Day 5	Day 6	Day 7
Often							
Sometimes							
Not at all							

＊ Also, at the end of each day this week, go over the events of the day from the moment you woke up till the present moment. Look at the day from the outside, so to speak, as a neutral observer would. Observe not just the external events but your inner reactions: your thoughts and feelings and fantasies and mood. Then move on to the next event and so forth through every portion of the day. Do not judge yourself or the event. Just look. No condemnation, no approval. Journal about it.

Notes to Myself: _____

_____

_____

_____

_____

_____

_____

_____

_____

_____

_____

_____

_____

_____

_____

WEEK 6

The root of suffering is attachment.

—The Buddha

The root cause of your suffering is attachment. What is an attachment? An attachment is an emotional state of clinging caused by the belief that without some thing or some person or some result you cannot be happy. Look at this society we live in, rotten to the core, infected as it is with attachments. It has programmed you to build your life on the unquestioned belief that without money, power, success, approval, a good reputation, romance, friendship, or God, you cannot be happy. Look at the heartache this breeds. Look at the loneliness in people, the fear in people, the confusion, the inner conflict, the outer conflict.

Yet in our culture, if anyone is attached to power, money, property, fame, and success, if anyone seeks these things as if their happiness depended on them, they will be considered productive members of society, dynamic and hardworking. If they pursue these things with a driving ambition that destroys the symphony of their life and makes them hard and cold and insensitive to others and to themselves, society will look upon them as dependable, and their relatives and friends will be proud of the status that they have achieved. How many so-called respectable people do you know who have retained the gentle sensitivity of love only unattachment offers? Understand, happiness isn't a thing, yet we have subtle ways of making our happiness depend on things within us and outside of us.

If you contemplate all this long enough, you will experience a disgust so deep that you will instinctively fling every attachment away as you would a serpent that has settled on you. You will revolt and break loose from this putrid culture that is based on acquisitiveness and attachment, on anxiety

33

and greed, and on the hardness and insensitivity of nonlove. Consider how we're enslaved by various attachments: we're striving to rearrange the world so that we can keep these attachments, because the world is a constant threat to them. We fear that a lover may stop loving us; he or she may turn to somebody else. We must keep making ourselves attractive because we have to seduce this other person. Somehow we were brainwashed into thinking we need his or her love. But we really don't. We don't need anybody's love; we just need to get in touch with reality. We need to break out of this prison of ours, this programming, this conditioning, these false beliefs, these fantasies; we need to break out into reality. Reality is lovely; it is an absolute delight. Eternal life is now. We're surrounded by it, like the fish in the ocean, but we have no notion about it at all. We're too distracted with our attachments.

> "We need to break out of this prison of ours, this programming, this conditioning, these false beliefs, these fantasies; we need to break out into reality."

Contrary to what your culture and religion have taught you, nothing—but absolutely nothing of the world—can make you happy. It is essential that you understand this because, until you do, there is no question of your ever finding the reality that is the kingdom of joy. The moment you see that absolutely nothing of the world can make you happy, you will stop moving from one job to another, one friend or lover to another, one place, one spiritual technique, one guru to another. None of these things can give you a single minute of happiness. They can only offer you a temporary thrill, a pleasure that inevitably turns into the fear of losing them, or pain if you should lose them, or boredom if you keep them. If we want to come awake—which is the same thing as saying if we want to love, if we want freedom, if we want joy and peace and spirituality—the first thing to understand is the root of our suffering is attachment.

Self-Observation

The rich industrialist from the North was horrified to find the Southern fisherman lying lazily beside his boat, smoking a pipe.

"Why aren't you out fishing?" said the industrialist.

"Because I have caught enough fish for the day," said the fisherman.

"Why don't you catch some more?"

"What would I do with it?"

"You could earn more money," was the reply. "With that you could have a motor fixed to your boat and go into deeper waters and catch more fish. Then you would make enough to buy nylon nets. These would bring you more fish and more money. Soon you would have enough money to own two boats . . . maybe even a fleet of boats. Then you would be a rich man like me."

"What would I do then?"

"Then you could really enjoy life."

"What do you think I am doing right now?"

From *The Song of the Bird*

THIS WEEK, FOCUS ON THE FOLLOWING:

✳ This week, review the simple steps to becoming aware presented in Week 5. Master these steps and use them each day throughout the day. Continue to track how often during the day you met negative thoughts and emotions with awareness.

Tracking How Consciously Aware You Are Becoming

Frequency	Day 1	Day 2	Day 3	Day 4	Day 5	Day 6	Day 7
Often							
Sometimes							
Not at all							

✳ Make a list of your attachments to people or things that you falsely believe you could not be happy without. Then take the statement "I cannot be happy unless or until" and fill in the blanks. Spend time seeing how each attachment is the cause of excitement and pleasure on the one hand and worry, insecurity, and unhappiness on the other. Can you see it as the root of your suffering? Journal about it.

I Cannot Be Happy Unless or Until

Notes to Myself: _____

_____

_____

_____

_____

_____

_____

_____

_____

_____

_____

_____

_____

_____

WEEK 7

History . . . is a nightmare from which I am trying to awake.

—James Joyce

Look carefully and you will see that the one and only thing that causes unhappiness is attachment. An attachment is a belief that without something or someone or some result you are not going to be happy. Once your attachment had you in its grip you began to strive might and main, every waking minute of your life, to rearrange the world around you so that you could attain and maintain the objects of your attachment. Think of someone gobbling up food in a concentration camp. With one hand, he gleefully brings the food to his mouth; with the other hand, he anxiously protects it from someone nearby who he fears will grab it from him the moment he lowers his guard. There you have the perfect image of the attached person. An attachment, by its very nature, makes you vulnerable to emotional turmoil and is always threatening to shatter your peace. To understand the degree of rigidity and deadness that attachments cause, you only need observe the amount of pain you experience when you lose a cherished idea, person, or thing. The pain and the grief betray your clinging, do they not? That is why when life bursts in to shatter the illusion inherent in attachments, you experience so much pain.

Each thing you cling to becomes a nightmare that causes you excitement and pleasure on the one hand but also worry, insecurity, tension, anxiety, fear, and unhappiness on the other. Father and mother? Nightmare. Wife and children, brothers and sisters? Nightmare. Money, job, and all your possessions? Nightmare. Your life as it is now? Nightmare. Every single thing you cling to and have convinced yourself you cannot live without? Nightmare.

How is an attachment formed? First, there's contact with something that gives you pleasure: a car, an attractively advertised device or appliance, a word of praise, or a person's company. There are even people who are attached to a pet theory, ideology, or belief. Then comes the desire to hold on to it and to repeat the gratifying sensation that the thing or person caused you. Finally comes the conviction that you will not be happy without that person or thing or result, for you have equated the pleasure it brings you with happiness. It is these two elements, the one positive—the flash of excitement, the thrill that you experience when you get what you are attached to—and the other negative, which is the sense of threat and tension at losing it that always accompanies the attachment. So how can you expect an attached person to enter that ocean of happiness called the kingdom of joy? As well as you can expect a camel to pass through the eye of a needle! The truth about the thrill is that it is only a temporary thrill that initially grows in intensity then turns into boredom after a while if you keep it. "Oh, I'm so thrilled, I've got it!" But how long does that last? A few minutes, a few days at the most. When you get your brand-new car, how long does the thrill last?

> **Attachment was programmed into you, stamped into the roots of your being, and once you were convinced of it as the only model for happiness, you were finished.**

Nobody told you this; they told you the opposite. Attachment is the only model you were given to be happy, despite the rigidity and deadness and unhappiness that attachments cause. Our culture, our society and, I'm sorry to say, even our religion gave you no other model. Attachment was programmed into you, stamped into the roots of your being, and once you were convinced of it as the only model for happiness, you were finished.

That's why you're in the mess that you're in right now. That is why you're asleep. There's only one way out and that is to get deprogrammed.

Self-Observation

One of Junaid's followers came to him with a purse full of gold coins. "Have you any more gold coins?" asked Junaid.

"Yes, many more."

"And you are attached to them?"

"I am."

"Then you must keep this too, for your need is greater than mine. Since I have nothing and desire nothing, I am much wealthier than you are, you see."

The heart of the enlightened is like a mirror: it grasps nothing, refuses nothing; it receives but does not keep.

From *The Heart of the Enlightened*

THIS WEEK, FOCUS ON THE FOLLOWING:

* Return to the list of attachments you made in Week 6. Choose one and detect whatever upset or pain this attachment causes you. Then reflect on how the pain it causes is the result of your clinging to either someone, something, or some outcome. Can you see this? Then choose another of your attachments, processing it in the same manner.

* Again this week, review the simple steps to becoming aware presented in Week 5. Master these steps and use them each day throughout the day, and continue to track how often during the day you met negative thoughts and emotions with awareness.

Tracking How Consciously Aware You Are Becoming

Frequency	Day 1	Day 2	Day 3	Day 4	Day 5	Day 6	Day 7
Often							
Sometimes							
Not at all							

NOTES TO MYSELF: _____

_____

_____

_____

_____

_____

_____

_____

_____

_____

_____

_____

_____

_____

_____

_____

WEEK 8

We need the compassion and the courage to change the conditions
that support our suffering. Those conditions are things like ignorance,
bitterness, negligence, clinging, and holding on.

—Sharon Salzberg

Hardly anyone has been told the following truth: in order to be genuinely happy, there is one and only one thing you need to do—get deprogrammed and get rid of those attachments. When people stumble upon this self-evident truth, they become terrified at the thought of the pain involved in dropping their attachments. But the process is not a painful one at all. On the contrary, getting rid of attachments is a perfectly delightful task—that is, if the instrument you use to rid yourself of them is not willpower or renunciation, but sight: the sight that the light of awareness restores. All you need to do is open your eyes and see that you do not really need the object of your attachment at all—that you were programmed, brainwashed by society into thinking that you could not be happy or you could not live without that person or thing or result. Not true.

> "An attachment is not a fact. It is a belief, a fantasy, a delusion programmed into your head by your culture."

Can you remember how upset you once were, certain you never would be happy again because you lost someone or something that was precious to you? But as time passed you got over it, didn't you? That should have alerted you to the falseness of your belief, to the trick your programmed mind was playing on you. An attachment is not a fact. It is a belief, a fantasy, a delusion programmed into your head by your culture. If that fantasy did not exist inside your head, you would not be attached.

Does the dropping of attachments mean detachment from the material world? No. One uses the material world, one enjoys the material world, but one doesn't make one's happiness depend on the material world. What I'm saying is, you really begin to enjoy things when you're unattached because attachment brings anxiety. If you're anxious when you're holding on to something, you can hardly be said to enjoy it. So, detachment is not a withdrawal from enjoyment. What this understanding is offering you is a way of transcending craving, anxiety, stress, disappointment, dissatisfaction, possessiveness, jealousy, and depression at the loss of something. You would love things and people and life, and you would enjoy them and appreciate them thoroughly, but on a nonattachment basis. In fact, is there any other way to really enjoy something?

Anyone who stops clinging to father, mother, wife, children, land, houses, things is repaid a hundred times over and gains eternal life. Then you will so easily take leave of your possessions—that is, you will stop clinging—and you will have destroyed clinging's capacity to hurt you. Then, at last, you will experience that mysterious state that cannot be described or uttered—the state of abiding happiness and peace called the kingdom of joy. Finding the kingdom of joy is the easiest thing in the world but also the most difficult. It's easy because it is all around you and within you, and all you have to do is reach out and take possession of it. It's difficult because if you wish to possess the kingdom, you can possess nothing else. That is, you must drop all inward leaning on any person or thing and forever withdraw from them the power to thrill you, excite you, or give you a feeling of security or well-being. Externally, everything will go on as before, but though you will continue to be *in* the world, you will no longer be *of* it. In your heart, you will now be free.

You probably think this is an unattainable ideal but there are people who have attained this. The only reason you too are not free is that your programming still stubbornly insists that reality be reshaped to conform to its demands.

Self-Observation

True philosopher that he was, Socrates believed that the wise person would instinctively lead a frugal life. He himself would not even wear shoes; yet he constantly fell under the spell of the marketplace and would go there often to look at all the wares on display. When one of his friends asked why, Socrates said, "I love to go there and discover how many things I am perfectly happy without."

From *The Heart of the Enlightened*

THIS WEEK, FOCUS ON THE FOLLOWING:

* Review various stages of your life—childhood, adolescence, adulthood, middle age—searching for things that seemed immeasurably important at each of these stages and that caused you worry and anxiety, things that you stubbornly clung to, things that you thought you could never live without. When you look back from the distance of today, how many of those loves, dreams, and fears still have the hold they had on you in former years? Then review some of the problems that you have today, the concerns of some of your present suffering, and of each of them say: "This, too, will pass away."

* One last time review the simple steps to becoming aware presented in Week 5. Master these steps, use them each day throughout

the day, and track how often during the day you met negative thoughts and emotions with awareness.

Tracking How Consciously Aware You Are Becoming

Frequency	Day 1	Day 2	Day 3	Day 4	Day 5	Day 6	Day 7
Often							
Sometimes							
Not at all							

NOTES TO MYSELF: _____

_____

_____

_____

_____

_____

_____

_____

_____

_____

_____

_____

_____

_____

WEEK 9

*Attachment to things drops away by itself when you
no longer seek to find yourself in them.*

—Eckhart Tolle

There is only one way to win the battle of attachments: drop them. Contrary to popular belief, dropping attachments is easy. All you have to do is see, but really see, the following truths.

First truth: You are holding on to a false belief, namely, the belief that without this particular person or thing you will not be happy. See the falseness of this belief. You may encounter resistance from your heart, but the moment you do see, there will be an immediate emotional result. At that very instant the attachment loses its force.

Second truth: If you just enjoy things, refusing to let yourself be attached to them, that is, refusing to hold the false belief that you will not be happy without them, you are spared all the struggle and emotional strain of protecting them and guarding them for yourself. Has it occurred to you that you can keep all the objects of your attachments without giving them up, without renouncing a single one of them, and you can enjoy them even more on a nonattachment, a non-clinging basis, because you are peaceful now and relaxed and unthreatened in your enjoyment of them?

The third and final truth: If you learn to enjoy the scent of a thousand flowers you will not cling to one or suffer when you cannot get it. If you have a thousand favorite dishes, the loss of one will go unnoticed and leave your happiness unimpaired. But it is precisely your attachments that prevent you from developing a wider and more varied taste for things and people.

In the light of these three truths, no attachment can survive. But the light must shine uninterruptedly if it is to be effective. Attachments can

> "…the transforming light of awareness brushes aside your scheming, self-seeking ego to give Nature full rein to bring about the kind of change that she produces in the rose: artless, graceful, unselfconscious, wholesome, untainted by inner conflict."

only thrive in the darkness of illusion. The rich man cannot enter the kingdom of joy not because he wants to be bad but because he chooses to be blind.

Will change occur then? Oh, yes. In you and in your surroundings. But it will not be brought about by your cunning, restless ego that is forever competing, comparing, coercing, sermonizing, manipulating in its intolerance and its ambitions, thereby creating tension and conflict and resistance between you and Nature—an exhausting, self-defeating process. No, the transforming light of awareness brushes aside your scheming, self-seeking ego to give Nature full rein to bring about the kind of change that she produces in the rose: artless, graceful, unselfconscious, wholesome, untainted by inner conflict.

✿

Self-Observation

Traveler: "What kind of weather are we going to have today?"
Shepherd: "The kind of weather I like."
"How do you know it will be the kind of weather you like?"

"Having found out, sir, that I cannot always get what I like, I have learned always to like what I get. So I am quite sure we will have the kind of weather I like."

From *The Prayer of the Frog*

THIS WEEK, FOCUS ON THE FOLLOWING:

* Spend time meditating on the kind of feeling that comes upon you when you're in touch with Nature or when you're absorbed in work that you love or when you're really conversing in openness and intimacy with someone you enjoy without any clinging. Those feelings are soul feelings.
* Now compare those feelings with the worldly feelings you have when you win an argument or when you prevail in a competition or when you make money or when everybody's applauding you. Journal about it.

Notes to Myself: _____

_____

_____

_____

_____

_____

_____

_____

_____

_____

_____

_____

_____

WEEK 10

Ego says, "Once everything falls into place, I'll find peace."
Spirit says, "Find your peace, and then everything will fall into place."
—Marianne Williamson

If you take a good look at the way you have been put together and the way you function, you will find that inside your head there is a whole program stamped into you, a set of demands about how the world should be, how you should be, and what you should want. Now, however old you are or wherever you go, your computer goes along with you and is active and operating at each conscious moment of the day. It is imperiously insisting that its demands be met by life, by people, and by you. If the demands are met, the computer allows you the only peace you can ever know—a temporary respite from negative emotions. If the demands are not met, even though it is no fault of yours, the computer generates negative emotions that cause you to suffer shame. It becomes a way of life. It is a pathetic existence that is constantly at the mercy of things and people as you try desperately to make life conform to your programming's demands.

In short, you've been trained to upset yourself. For instance, when other people don't live up to your computer's expectations, it torments you with frustration, anger, or bitterness. When things are not under your control, or the future is uncertain, your computer insists that you experience anxiety, tension, or worry. Then you expend a lot of energy coping with these negative emotions by expending even more energy trying to rearrange the world around you so that the demands of your computer will be met. If that happens, you will be granted a measure of precarious peace; it's precarious because at any moment, some trifle—a plane delay, a device that doesn't work, a document that hasn't arrived, a spot on your tie or blouse,

57

you name it—is going to be out of conformity with your computer's programming, and the computer will insist that you become upset again.

Who is responsible for the programming?

Not you. Would anyone in their right mind sit down and knowingly and willingly and deliberately upset themselves? It isn't really you who decided even such basics as your wants, desires, and so-called needs, your values, your tastes, and your attitudes. It was your parents, your society, your culture, your religion, and your past experiences that fed the operating instructions into your computer.

These things depend on the criteria society establishes; they depend on your social conditioning that was stamped into you. You've been programmed with this. You've been conditioned this way. This is what you've got to understand. These things in you that you struggle to fix just need to be understood. If you understood them, they would change.

> "It was your parents, your society, your culture, your religion, and your past experiences that fed the operating instructions into your computer."

You see, you don't have to do anything for enlightenment. You don't have to do anything for liberation and spirituality. All you have to do is see something, understand something. If you would understand it, you would be free.

Self-Observation

"Where shall I look for Enlightenment?"

"Here."

"When will it happen?"

"It is happening right now."

"Then why don't I experience it?"

"Because you do not look."

"What should I look for?"

"Nothing. Just look."

"At what?"

"Anything your eyes alight upon."

"Must I look in a special kind of way?"

"No. The ordinary way will do."

"But don't I always look the ordinary way?"

"No."

"Whyever not?"

"Because to look you must be here. You're mostly somewhere else."

From *One Minute Wisdom*

THIS WEEK, FOCUS ON THE FOLLOWING:

* Think of a person or situation that upset you recently. Make it vivid by remembering the time and place where it happened, the thoughts you were thinking, and the emotion you felt. Journal about the situation. Once you have it clear in your mind, ask yourself this: Did you think this person or event was to blame for your upset? Or did you think you were to blame and brought on

the upset yourself? Now look at how you have been programmed to react this way. Journal about it.

* This week, be keenly aware of situations that arise in which you get upset because you didn't get what you wanted, or when a situation was not under your control, or when something happened that made your future feel uncertain to you. Notice how something within you insists that you become upset from the belief that this is not what should happen and see through it to the social conditioning that insists you become upset. Journal about this too.

NOTES TO MYSELF: _____

_____

_____

_____

_____

_____

_____

_____

_____

_____

_____

_____

_____

_____

WEEK 11

I hope for nothing. I fear nothing. I am free.

—Nikos Kazantzakis

Does "no attachment" mean that we should not participate in the very human, creative endeavors of hoping and dreaming and doing your best? Not at all. What no attachment represents is a new attitude for engaging the world. It's a willing attitude that says, "I want to be aware; I want to be in touch with whatever is and let whatever happens happen." It is adjusting to the understanding that the moment you make a goal out of something and attempt to get it, you're seeking ego glorification, ego promotion, and life goes out of the endeavor. There's a lovely account from Tranxu, a great Chinese sage, which goes: "When the archer shoots for no particular prize, he has all his skills. When he shoots to win a brass buckle, he is already nervous. When he shoots for a gold prize, he goes blind, sees two targets, and is out of his mind. His skill has not changed, but the prize divides him. He cares! He thinks more of winning than of shooting, and the need to win drains him of power." Isn't that an image of most people?

> When you're living for nothing, you've got all your skills, you've got all your energy, you're relaxed, and you don't care.

When you're living for nothing, you've got all your skills, you've got all your energy, you're relaxed, and you don't care. It doesn't matter to you whether you win or lose. That's the difference.

Now there's human living for you. That's what life is all about. No one joins in the human enterprise of human dreams and visions and goals so marvelously and so creatively as the person who is unattached. Yet, lots of people cannot even conceive of swinging into action without first upsetting themselves. The mystics and the prophets didn't bother one bit about honor or disgrace. Honor or disgrace, success or failure meant nothing to them.

They were living in another world, the world of the awakened. Unfortunately, we've come to associate nonattachment with not caring, with not enjoying, with asceticism. I'm not talking about that at all.

There is another question related to nonattachment that is a hard one to take in and you may need time to digest it. The question is, if you loved someone and were not attached to that person, would you grieve if you were to lose them? You would not grieve if you had not made them your happiness. But rather if you enjoyed them wholly, you loved them in the sense of "I was sensitive, I cared, it was their good I saw, I left them to be free," then you would not have given over to them the power to decide whether you will be happy or not. In that case, you would not grieve at their absence or at their rejection or at their death. If you do grieve, it can be wonderful. Grief when embraced can gradually drain the heartache out of you, after which you come back to life again.

Self-Observation

When the archer shoots for no particular prize, he has all his skills. When he shoots to win a brass buckle, he is already nervous. When he shoots for a gold prize . . . the prize divides him. . . . He thinks more of winning than of shooting, and the need to win drains him of power.

From *Awareness*

THIS WEEK, FOCUS ON THE FOLLOWING:

* As you face challenges and swing into action this week, first reflect on the wisdom in the passage above about the archer from the Chinese sage Tranxu and apply it to the situation.

* Journal about when you were challenged to perform well, and the effect on you in choosing to be mindful to *shoot for no particular prize or outcome*, or the effect when you *shoot to win the brass buckle*, metaphorically speaking, or when you shoot even higher, for the *gold prize*. Journal about the difference in experience between functioning from each of these three attitudes.

NOTES TO MYSELF: _____

_____

_____

_____

_____

_____

_____

_____

_____

_____

_____

_____

_____

WEEK 12

The mystics keep trying to tell us that reality is all right. The upset is in you, not in reality. Reality is not problematic. Problems exist only in the human mind. We might add "in the ignorant, programmed, conditioned, sleeping mind." Reality is not problematic, but most people are not ready to hear that.

What decides what will finally make its way to your conscious mind from all the material that is pouring in from the world?

Three decisive filters:

* First, your attachments.
* Second, your beliefs.
* Third, your fears.

Your attachments: You will inevitably look for what fosters or threatens them and turn a blind eye to the rest. You won't be interested in the rest any more than the avaricious businessperson is interested in anything that does not involve the making of money.

Your beliefs: Just take a look at a fanatic who only notices what confirms his or her belief and blocks out whatever threatens it and you will understand what your beliefs are doing to you.

And then your fears: If you knew you were to be executed in a week's time it would wonderfully concentrate your mind to the exclusion of everything else. That is what fears do; they irresistibly rivet your attention

> **You falsely think that your fears protect you, your beliefs have made you what you are, and your attachments make your life exciting and secure.**

on to some things to the exclusion of others.

The people who trained us, the people who programmed us, feared that if we didn't upset ourselves, we wouldn't do anything. It never occurred to them that when you upset yourself, you have less energy to do something and perception is distorted. You're not seeing things right anymore. You're overreacting.

You falsely think that your fears protect you, your beliefs have made you what you are, and your attachments make your life exciting and secure. You fail to see that fear is actually a screen between you and life's symphony.

Self-Observation

A frog had lived all his life in a well. One day he was surprised to see another frog there.

"Where have you come from?" he asked.

"From the sea. That's where I live," said the other.

"What's the sea like? Is it big as my well?"

The sea frog laughed. "There's no comparison," he said.

The well frog pretended to be interested in what his visitor had to say about the sea. But he thought, Of all the liars I have known in my lifetime, this one is undoubtedly the greatest—and the most shameless!

How does one speak of the ocean to a frog in the well; or of Reality to the ideologue?

From *The Prayer of the Frog*

THIS WEEK, FOCUS ON THE FOLLOWING:

* **Attachment:** Journal about someone or something you think you cannot be happy without. Feel the grasping and clinging this produces and how it upsets you and narrows your perspective, causing you to turn a blind eye to the rest of life.
* **Belief:** Journal about a political or spiritual belief you hold and see how it causes you to only notice what confirms your belief and blocks out whatever threatens it.
* **Fear:** List ways in which you think fear protects you. Then recall a concrete example of when you were fearful of someone or something. What toll did fear take on your energy and your clarity? How did it distort the way you perceived people and events? How did it cause you to overreact? Journal about this.

Notes to Myself: _____

_____

_____

_____

_____

_____

_____

_____

_____

_____

_____

_____

_____

_____

WEEK 13

Heaven itself is reached with empty hands and open minds, which come
with nothing to find everything and claim it as their own.

—A Course in Miracles

Whenever you are anxious and afraid, it is because you might fail to get
or are afraid of losing the object of your attachment. And any time you
feel jealous, isn't it because someone might make off with what you are
attached to? Almost all of your anger comes from someone standing in the
way of your attachment, doesn't it? See how paranoid you become when
your attachment is threatened? You can't think objectively. Your whole
vision becomes distorted, doesn't it? Every time you feel bored, isn't it
because you are not getting a sufficient supply of what you are attached to,
meaning some thrill you believe will make you happy? Did you think happiness was excitement or thrills? You're thrilled but there is anxiety behind
it: the anxiety of *how can I make it last*? You know you can't and that's
what causes the depression. Didn't anyone tell you that? You're thrilled, all
right, but you're just preparing the way for your next depression. That's
not happiness, that's addiction.

And when you are depressed and miserable, the cause is that life is not
giving you what you have convinced yourself you can't be happy without.

If your spirit becomes unclogged from these filters and your senses
open you will begin to perceive things as they really are and to interact with
reality and you will be entranced by the harmonies of the universe. Then
you will understand what God is, for you will at last know what love is.

You see persons and things not as they are but as you are. If you wish
to see them as they are you must attend to your attachments and the fears
that your attachments generate. Because when you look at life it is these

attachments, beliefs, and fears that will decide what you will notice and what you block out. Whatever you notice then commands your attention. And since your looking has been selective, you have an illusory version of the things and people around you. The more you live with this distorted version, the more you become convinced that it is the true picture of the world because your attachments and fears continue to process incoming data in a way that will reinforce your picture.

This is what gives origin to your beliefs: fixed, unchanging ways of looking at a reality that is not fixed and unchanging at all but is movement and change. So, it is no longer the real world that you interact with and love but a world created by your head. It is only when you drop your beliefs, your fears, and the attachments that breed them that you will be freed from the insensitivity that makes you so deaf and blind to yourself and to the world.

> It is only when you drop your beliefs, your fears, and the attachments that breed them that you will be freed from the insensitivity that makes you so deaf and blind to yourself and to the world.

As you begin to understand this, you stop making demands of yourself, of other people, and of the world. You stop having expectations of yourself and the world. You stop pushing. If you could get one second's experience of that, you'd be breaking through your prison and getting a glimpse of the sky. Someday, maybe, you will even fly.

Self-Observation

A man came to Buddha with an offering of flowers in his hands. Buddha looked up at him and said, "Drop it!"

He couldn't believe he was being asked to drop the flowers. But then it occurred to him that he was probably being invited to drop the flowers he had in his left hand, since to offer something with one's left hand was considered inauspicious and impolite. So he dropped the flowers that his left hand held.

Still Buddha said, "Drop it!"

Perplexed, the man asked, "What is it I am supposed to drop?"

"Not the flowers, son, but the one who brought them," was Buddha's reply.

From *The Prayer of the Frog*

THIS WEEK, FOCUS ON THE FOLLOWING:

✳ As you relate to people and events, remind yourself that, in truth, you see persons and things not as they are but as you are. Then consider that if you wish to see them as they are you must attend to your attachments, fears, and beliefs, because otherwise they will command your attention, deciding what you will notice and what you block out.

✳ Step back from your attachment, fears, and beliefs and see how they have built a prison around you, and how dropping them frees you. You stop making demands of yourself, of other people, and of the world. You stop having expectations of yourself and the world. Think of an attachment you currently hold on to that causes you distress. Imagine tying this attachment to a helium balloon and watching it lift-up into the air, disappearing from sight. Then bring your attention to this moment, right here and now, and open up to all that you have, every blessing in your life.

Notes to Myself: _____

_____

_____

_____

_____

_____

_____

_____

_____

_____

_____

_____

_____

_____

_____

_____

_____

_____

_____

_____

_____

_____

_____

_____

_____

_____

_____

_____

_____

WEEK 14

Wanna fly, you got to give up the shit that weighs you down.

—Toni Morrison

Get yourself ready for a shock. Here it comes: Nothing in reality, nothing in life, nothing in the world upsets you. Nothing has the power to upset you. All upset exists in you, not in reality. All upset is in you, not in life. For most people, life is something that happens to them while they're busy suffering all sorts of other things. Here's one image of this: Think of a concert hall. The orchestra is to play a symphony. You've settled nice and comfortably in your seat and you're ready to enjoy the music,

> All upset is in you, not in life. For most people, life is something that happens to them while they're busy suffering all sorts of other things.

then suddenly you remember that you forgot to lock your car. Oh no, what do you do now? You can't get out—it'll be too disturbing to others. You feel trapped and you cannot enjoy the music because you're ruminating about your car. That is the image of life for most people. Constant anxiety. *What do I do now? What's going to happen next? How do I cope with this? How do I deal with that?* There is another way of relating to life.

Let's get concrete about this. Begin with your being upset. What is it that upset you? Has somebody died? Has somebody betrayed you? Has someone rejected you? You lost something? Your plans have gone awry? You didn't achieve the outcome you wanted? Whatever.

81

Just understanding this has changed people's lives. It turns them around 180 degrees. Just understanding this, and nothing more. Reality is not upsetting. Reality is not problematic. All problems exist in the human mind. Somebody once said to me, "Surely there must be some problems that exist in reality and not in me?" I said to him, "If we take you out of the situation, where's the problem?" No you, no problem. People think that the problem exists in the world. They think that it exists in other people. They think that it is in life. No, no, no. It's in them.

Let's work this out. Somebody broke a promise and you're upset. What do you think upset you? The broken promise? I could bring another individual here in your place who is also faced with a broken promise but is not upset. How come you got upset? Now, you were trained into habitually thinking that it was the broken promise that upset you. It was your programming. It was your training. You've been trained to upset yourself every time you're faced with a broken promise.

Here is another example. You're planning a picnic and the picnic gets rained out and you're upset. Where do you think the upset is—in the rain or in your reaction to the rain? The rain is neutral; it is just what is. Someone else would see it this way and not be upset. If you had not made your happiness depend on its not raining, you wouldn't be upset either. But you and I have been trained to make our happiness depend on certain things, and so when those things don't happen, thanks to our programming, we upset ourselves.

Self-Observation

The Japanese warrior was captured by his enemies and thrown into prison. At night he could not sleep for he was convinced that he would be tortured the next morning.

Then the words of his master came to his mind. "Tomorrow is not real. The only reality is now."

So he came to the present—and fell asleep.

From *The Song of the Bird*

THIS WEEK, FOCUS ON THE FOLLOWING:

✳ Think of something that upset you recently. Now consider that it wasn't that thing or that person that upset you. It was your programming. Thus, it wasn't someone's meanness or disapproval or rejection; it wasn't some outside condition. It was your programming that upset you. So, it makes no sense to blame yourself or other people or circumstances. Shift the way you relate to the upset and see what happens to you.

✳ Throughout this week follow the two steps below. Do it repeatedly, again and again, whenever you are upset:

The first step is awareness: "Gee, this thing upset me."

The second step is understanding: "Wait a second, it wasn't this thing that upset me; it was my programming that upset me. So, there is nothing to attack or defend against or blame. There is just this upset to bring into awareness and allow to pass."

NOTES TO MYSELF: _____

_____

_____

_____

_____

_____

_____

_____

_____

_____

_____

_____

_____

_____

WEEK 15

I have given you authority to tread on serpents and scorpions,
and over all the power of the enemy, and nothing shall hurt you.

—Jesus Christ

Let's carry last week's theme into this week, namely that nothing in this entire world has the power to upset you and that nothing has ever upset you. Nobody has ever hurt you. I know I'm repeating myself, but it's important. So, if that is true, then it follows that "they" didn't hurt me, reality didn't hurt me. Thus it makes no sense to lash out against him or her or it.

So, where does my upset come from? Was it me? Was it me hurting me? If that's it, then I'm going to lash out against me. "Why do I do this to me?" I'll moan to myself. Next I'll be getting angry with me. I'm getting upset with me. I'm going to hate me for the way I am.

Well, I've got good news for you. They didn't do it to you. The world didn't do it to you. Life didn't do it to you. And best of all, you didn't do it to you. In your right mind would you knowingly and willingly and deliberately upset yourself? So, stop blaming yourself.

Then who did it?

It's your programming. You've been programmed to upset yourself. You've been conditioned this way. This is what your society and culture did to you, and I'm sorry to say, your religion. This has been stamped into you. This is what you've got to understand.

Has it ever struck you that you have been programmed by society to be unhappy, and so, no matter what you do to become happy, you are bound to fail?

When other people or outcomes don't live up to your programmed expectations, you're programmed to torment yourself with frustration, anger, or bitterness. As was stated before, people often do not realize how unhappy they have been until they experience a spontaneous moment of joy. If you wish to be happy, if you wish to be at peace, the first thing you need isn't effort or even goodwill or good desires. You need a clear understanding of exactly how you have been programmed.

> "You know, one of the signs of maturity is when you no longer blame anyone. You don't blame others; you don't blame yourself. You see what's wrong, and you set about remedying it.

"I'm upset. I've upset myself. They did it to me." Wrong.

"So then I did it to myself." Wrong.

It's your programming that's doing it to you. It's the culture that's doing it to you. This is the way you've been brought up; this is the way you've been trained. This is what you've got to understand. You know, one of the signs of maturity is when you no longer blame anyone. You don't blame others; you don't blame yourself. You see what's wrong, and you set about remedying it. That's one fairly good sign of maturity. The remedy to the problem of the way you have been programmed is awareness. What you are aware of, you control; what you are unaware of controls you.

Self-Observation

An elderly woman who was an enthusiastic gardener declared that she had no faith whatsoever in predictions that someday scientists would learn to control the weather. According to her, all that was needed to control the weather was prayer.

Then one summer, while she was away on a foreign trip, a drought hit the land and wiped out her entire garden. She was so upset when she got back that she changed her religion.

From *The Prayer of the Frog*

THIS WEEK, FOCUS ON THE FOLLOWING:

* Imagine your social programming is a radio that, no matter how you turn the knob, picks up only one station broadcasting negative content through which you become upset. Imagine you have no control over the volume. At times the sound is barely audible; at others, it is so loud that it almost shatters your eardrums. Moreover, the radio is impossible to turn off; at times it will be slow, then it will suddenly begin to blare away when you want to rest and sleep. Who would put up with this kind of performance in a radio? And yet you have been programmed to behave in this crazy fashion, and you not only put up with it, but regard it as normal and human.

* Now imagine that one day through some act of grace the radio suddenly turns off and stops broadcasting. To your great relief all the noise is gone and the atmosphere in and around you fills with peace and quiet. Imagine that and journal about it.

Notes to Myself: _____

_____

_____

_____

_____

_____

_____

_____

_____

_____

_____

_____

_____

_____

WEEK 16

People don't live or die, people just float.
—Bob Dylan

Spirituality means waking up. But most people, even though they don't know it, are asleep. They're born asleep, live asleep, and die in their sleep without ever waking up. Most people are so brainwashed that they do not even realize how unhappy they are. They never understand the loveliness and the beauty of this thing that we call human existence. It's only when they make contact with joy that they understand how depressed they had been. Has it ever struck you that you have been programmed by society to be unhappy, and so, no matter what you do to become happy, you are bound to fail? If you wish to awaken, if you wish to be happy, the first thing you need isn't effort or even goodwill or good desires. You need a clear understanding of exactly how you have been programmed.

> **Most people are so brainwashed that they do not even realize how unhappy they are. It's only when they make contact with joy that they understand how depressed they had been.**

Here is what happened to you: First your society and your culture taught you to believe that you would not be happy without certain persons, certain results, certain possessions. Once you swallowed this belief, you naturally developed an attachment to some person or thing or outcome and you were convinced that, without it, you could not be happy. Then followed your efforts to acquire your precious thing or person, to cling to it once it was acquired, and to fight off every possibility of losing it. This finally led you to abject emotional dependence so that the object of your attachment had the power to thrill you when you attained it, to make you anxious lest you be deprived of it, and to make you miserable when you lost it. Once your attachment had you in its grip, you began to strive with every waking minute of your life to rearrange the world around you so that you could attain and maintain the objects of your attachment. This is an exhausting task. It leaves you little energy for the business of living and enjoying life fully. It is also an impossible task in an ever-changing world that you simply are not able to control.

So, instead of living a life of serenity and fulfillment, you are doomed to a life of frustration, anxiety, worry, insecurity, suspense, and tension. For a few fleeting moments, the world does indeed yield to your efforts and rearranges itself to suit your desires. Then you experience a flash of pleasure and become what you regard as happy, briefly. But it isn't happiness at all because it is accompanied by the underlying fear that at any moment this world of things and people that you have painstakingly put in place will slip out of your control and let you down. And sooner or later, it will.

Why haven't we seen this; why haven't we learned from the suffering attachments cause? It is because we don't want to wake up to the truth that we really don't want happiness. We want *things*. Be honest enough to admit that to yourself.

It's not our fault. We have been programmed to want things and to believe we derive our happiness from people, things, and outcomes. It's as ridiculous as believing happiness is a smooth complexion, whiter teeth, or styled hair. If you'd only look you'd see that it is all based on a belief that without this or that, you cannot be happy. That's false. The moment you see that, you're free. It may take you one minute to see it; it may take you years. But the day you see it, you're free as a bird. Even if you're making an ass of yourself, it won't bother you. You're free. You won't be fazed one bit. You won't bother any longer to win others' approval or worry about rejection. You're completely free. It's so important that you understand that.

Self-Observation

"Don't look for God," the Master said. "Just look—and all will be revealed."

"But how is one to look?"

"Each time you look at anything, see only what is there and nothing else." The disciples were bewildered, so the Master made it simpler: "For instance: When you look at the moon, see the moon and nothing else."

"What else could one see except the moon when one looks at the moon?"

"A hungry person could see a ball of cheese. A lover, the face of his beloved."

From *One Minute Wisdom*

THIS WEEK, FOCUS ON THE FOLLOWING:

* Review the list of attachments you made in Week 6 and see which of the attachments you are still convinced that you cannot be happy without. Question that belief.
* Then acknowledge that right here, right now, you have everything you need to be happy, and that the only reason you are ever unhappy is because you are focused on what you don't have. Journal about the shift in experience this opens you to.

Notes to Myself: _____

_____

_____

_____

_____

_____

_____

_____

_____

_____

_____

_____

_____

WEEK 17

What do you have to do to acquire happiness? You don't have to do anything to acquire happiness because happiness cannot be acquired. Why? Because you have it already. How can you acquire what you already have? Uninterrupted happiness is uncaused. True happiness is uncaused. No person or thing makes you happy. Happiness is your natural state. Happiness is the natural state of little children to whom the kingdom belongs until they have been polluted and contaminated by the stupidity of society and culture.

One could use other words to define happiness, like peace, love, enlightenment, enjoying every moment as it occurs, living in the present. We have a natural urge to be free, a natural urge to be creative, and a natural urge to love and be happy and at peace. Think of it this way: your natural state of being is like the sky that clouds pass over. Clouds come and go, some dark, some white, but the sky remains. Many mystics and masters have said that before enlightenment, they identified themselves with the clouds. After enlightenment, they identified themselves with the sky. There was a great Zen master who had attained enlightenment, and one day his disciples said to him, "Master, what did you get from enlightenment?" And he said, "Before I was enlightened, I used to be depressed. After I got enlightened, I continued to be depressed." Puzzling isn't it? Attitude is the difference. You see, the depression didn't change; his attitude toward the depression changed. He's not saying, "I'm not going to be happy until this depression goes away." Because, strange as it may seem, you could even be serene and calm and happy while the depression is going on. You're not fighting it, you're not upset about it, you're not irritated about it. You're serene. That's the difference.

We understand so little about our own true nature, but this much is clear—that innately one does possess a state of serenity, of happiness, of freedom, of fulfillment, even as clouds pass. We were born happy. We lost it. We were born with the gift of life. We lost it. We've got to rediscover it. The great Meister Eckhart said, "God is not attained by a process of addition to anything in the soul, but by a process of subtraction." To rediscover what you truly are you have to drop something. You've got to drop attachments. You won't know what you are and what happiness is until attachment desires are dropped. Then you will know; then you will see.

> You only have to look and see that the attachment is based on a false belief that without this or that, you cannot be happy. The moment you see that belief is false, it drops, and you are free.

How does one drop attachments? Through awareness. You only have to look and see that the attachment is based on a false belief that without this or that, you cannot be happy. The moment you see that belief is false, it drops, and you are free. Again, you don't have to add anything in order to be happy; you've got to drop attachments. Then you're happy. So, stop wasting your energy trying to cure your baldness, building up an attractive body, or changing your job, your lifestyle, or your personality. Deep down, you know you could change every one of these things and still be unhappy.

Self-Observation

A man who took great pride in his lawn found himself with a large crop of dandelions. He tried every method he knew to get rid of them. Still they plagued him.

Finally he wrote the Department of Agriculture. He enumerated all the things he had tried and closed his letter with the question: "What shall I do now?"

In due course the reply came: "We suggest you learn to love them."

From *The Song of the Bird*

THIS WEEK, FOCUS ON THE FOLLOWING:

* Make a list of all the things you want to change about yourself, such as your appearance, your personality, your job, your social status, your place of residence, your spiritual resolve.
* Look over the list. Can you see that you could change every one of these things and still be dissatisfied and unhappy? Journal about this.

NOTES TO MYSELF: _____

_____

_____

_____

_____

_____

_____

_____

_____

_____

_____

_____

_____

WEEK 18

Blessed are the pure in heart, for they shall see God.

—Jesus Christ

Compare the serene and simple splendor of a rose in bloom with the tensions and restlessness of your life. The rose has a gift that you have lost: it is perfectly content to be itself. It has not been programmed from birth, as you have been, to be dissatisfied with itself, so it has not the slightest urge to be anything other than what it is. That is why it possesses the artless grace and absence of inner conflict that among humans is only found in little children and mystics.

Consider your sad condition. You are always dissatisfied with yourself, always wanting to change yourself. You suffer when you compare yourself with others who you see have achieved what you have not and have become what you are not. So, you are full of violence and self-intolerance which only grows with every effort that you make to change yourself. Any change you achieve is always accompanied by struggle and conflict. Would you be tormented by jealousy and envy if, like the rose, you were content to be what you are and never aspired to what you are not? But you are driven, are you not, to be like

> "You are always dissatisfied with yourself, always wanting to change yourself. You suffer when you compare yourself with others who you see have achieved what you have not and have become what you are not."

105

someone else who has more knowledge than you, better looks than you, more admiration and success than you. You want greater worldly success, don't you? Spiritually, you want to become more loving, more peaceful; you want to find God; you want to come closer to your ideals. Take a moment and think of the sad history of your efforts at self-improvement, which either ended in disaster or succeeded only at the cost of struggle and pain.

Now suppose you desisted from all efforts to change yourself and from all self-dissatisfaction. Would you then be doomed to go to sleep having passively accepted everything in you and around you? There is another way besides laborious self-pushing on the one hand and stagnant acceptance on the other. It is the way of awareness, the way of self-observation clearing the way to self-understanding. This is far from easy because to understand the truth of what you are requires complete freedom from all desire to change what you are into something else. You will see this if you compare the attitude of a scientist who studies the habits of ants without the slightest desire to change them. If what you attempt is not to change yourself but to observe yourself, to study every one of your reactions to people and things and the world, without judgment or condemnation or desire to reform yourself, your observation will be nonselective, comprehensive, never fixed on rigid conclusions, always open and fresh from moment to moment. Then you will notice a marvelous thing happening within you: You will be flooded with the light of awareness; you will become transparent and transformed. And you will be delighted to discover that for growth and transformation, it is enough simply to be watchful and awake. Will awareness bring you the holiness you so desire? True holiness, the type that is not achieved through techniques and efforts and repression, is completely unselfconscious. You wouldn't have the slightest awareness of its existence in you. Besides, you will not care, for even the ambition to be holy will have dropped as you live from moment to moment a life made full and happy and transparent through awareness. In this state your eyes will see the Savior, and nothing else, but absolutely nothing else will matter anymore.

Self-Observation

"Is there anything I can do to make myself Enlightened?"

"As little as you can do to make the sun rise in the morning."

"Then of what use are the spiritual exercises you prescribe?"

"To make sure you are not asleep when the sun begins to rise."

From *One Minute Wisdom*

THIS WEEK, FOCUS ON THE FOLLOWING:

* Imagine what it would feel like to no longer be dissatisfied with yourself, to no longer struggle to change yourself, but to accept yourself unconditionally, strengths, flaws, and all, without condemnation and without the need for anyone's approval or acceptance. Journal about it.

* Describe how you see your awareness practice developing. How has it changed you thus far? Journal about it.

NOTES TO MYSELF: _____

_____

_____

_____

_____

_____

_____

_____

_____

_____

_____

_____

_____

WEEK 19

We can open a sealed door in us and find that Something which will change the whole significance of life.

—Mirra Alfassa

If you wish to love, you must learn to see again. And if you wish to see, you must learn to give up your dependency and addictions. Tear away the tentacles of society that have enveloped and suffocated your being. You must drop them. Externally, everything will go on as before, but though you will continue to be in the world, you will no longer be of it. In your heart, you will now be free at last, if utterly alone. Your dependence on your attachments and addictions will die. You don't have to go to the desert; you're right in the middle of people; you're enjoying them immensely. But they no longer have the power to make you happy or miserable. That's what aloneness means. In this solitude your dependence dies. The capacity to love is born. One no longer sees others as means of satisfying one's addiction.

Only someone who has attempted this knows the terrors of the process. It's like inviting yourself to die. It's like asking the poor drug addict to give up the only happiness he has ever known. His challenge is replacing his drug with the wholesome taste of bread and fruit and the clean taste of the morning air, the sweetness of the water of the mountain stream. But while he is struggling with withdrawal and the emptiness now that his drug is gone, it will seem that nothing can fill the emptiness except the drug. Much the same challenge confronts you as you try to imagine a life in which you refuse to enjoy or take pleasure in a single word of appreciation or to rest your head on anyone's shoulder for support or to allow your happiness to depend on any outcome. Think of a life in which you depend on no one emotionally, so that no one has the power to make you happy or miserable anymore. You refuse to need any particular person for your happiness, or to be special to anyone, or to call anyone your own. You refuse to need any particular thing or results to be happy. The birds of the air have their nests and the foxes their holes, but you will have nowhere to rest your head in your journey through life. If you ever get to this state, you will at last know what it means to see with a vision that is clear and unclouded by fear or desire. Every word there is measured. You will know what it means to love. But to come to the land of love, you must pass through the pains of death, for to love people means to die to the need for people. To come home to yourself means to be utterly alone.

> **Think of a life in which you depend on no one emotionally, so that no one has the power to make you happy or miserable anymore.**

How would you ever get home? By a ceaseless awareness, by the infinite patience and compassion for yourself that you would have for a drug addict. By developing a taste for the good things in life to counter the craving for the drug called attachment. What good things? It's the love of work which you enjoy doing for the love of itself; the love of laughter and intimacy with people to whom you do not cling and on whom you do not depend emotionally but whose company you enjoy and whose beauty you see. It's giving time to activities that you can do with your whole being, activities that you so love to do that while you're engaged in them time stands still and success, recognition, and approval mean nothing. It's returning to Nature, sending the crowds away, and walking with God, silently communing with trees and flowers and animals and birds, with mountains and sea and clouds and sky and stars.

Self-Observation

Given the nature of the spiritual quest . . .

A man came upon a tall tower and stepped inside to find it all dark. As he groped around, he came upon a circular staircase. Curious to know where it led to, he began to climb, and as he climbed, he sensed a growing uneasiness in his heart. So he looked behind him and was horrified to see that each time he climbed a step, the previous one fell off and disappeared. Before him, the stairs wound upward and he had no idea where they led; behind him yawned an enormous black emptiness.

From *The Heart of the Enlightened*

THIS WEEK, FOCUS ON THE FOLLOWING:

* Take time this week to sit in solitude and imagine how it would feel if you stopped depending on others emotionally, so that no one had the power to make you happy or miserable anymore, where the power to be happy came from within you and nowhere else. Journal about it.
* Make time for one or more activities that you can do with your whole being, activities that you love to do.

NOTES TO MYSELF: _____

_____

_____

_____

_____

_____

_____

_____

_____

_____

_____

_____

_____

_____

WEEK 20

Getting where you want to be has everything to do with awareness, and
nothing to do with willpower.

—Cheri Huber

Spirituality is never achieved through effort and techniques. Nor are they commodities that one can buy or a prize that one can win. It is not what you do that brings them to you; Holiness is the essence of what you are and are becoming increasingly. That's what matters. Holiness is not an achievement; it is a grace. A grace called awareness, a grace called looking, observing, understanding. If you would only switch on the light of awareness and observe yourself and everything around you throughout the day, if you would see yourself reflected in the mirror of awareness the way you see your face reflected in a looking glass—that is, accurately, clearly, exactly as it is without the slightest distortion or addition—and if you observed this reflection without any judgment or condemnation, you would experience all sorts of marvelous changes coming about in you. Only you will not be in control of those changes, or be able to plan them in advance, or decide how and when they are to take place. It is this nonjudgmental awareness alone that heals and changes and makes one grow. But in its own way and at its own time.

> "If you would only switch on the light of awareness and observe yourself and everything around you throughout the day... you would experience all sorts of marvelous changes coming about in you."

117

What specifically are you to be aware of? Your reactions and your relationships. Each time you are in the presence of a person, any person, or with Nature or with any situation, you have all sorts of reactions, positive and negative. Study those reactions, observe what exactly they are and where they come from, without any sermonizing or guilt or even any desire, much less effort, to change them. That is all that one needs for holiness to arise.

Often I'm asked, "Isn't awareness itself an effort?" Not if you have tasted it even once. For then you will understand that awareness is a delight, the delight of a little child moving out in wonder to discover the world. For even when awareness uncovers unpleasant things in you, it always brings liberation and joy. Then you will understand why it is said that the unaware life is not worth living. It is too full of darkness and pain. You will then understand that awareness involves as much effort as a lover makes to go to his beloved, or a hungry man makes to eat his food, or a mountaineer to reach the top of the mountain; so much energy expended, so much hardship weathered, but it isn't effort, it's fun! In other words, awareness is an effortless activity.

Self-Observation

The mystic was back from the desert. "Tell us," the people said, "what God is like."

But how could he ever tell them what he had experienced in his heart? Can God be put into words?

He finally gave them a formula—so inaccurate, so inadequate— in the hope that some of them might be tempted to experience it themselves.

They seized upon the formula. They made it a sacred text.

They imposed it on others as a holy belief.

They went to great pains to spread it to foreign lands. Some even gave their lives for it.

The mystic was sad. It might have been better if he had said nothing.

From *The Song of the Bird*

THIS WEEK, FOCUS ON THE FOLLOWING:

* In practicing awareness this week, whenever you find yourself condemning yourself or approving of yourself, don't stop the condemnation and don't stop the judgment or approval; just watch it, such as, *I'm condemning me; I'm disapproving of me; I'm approving of me.* Just look at it, period. Don't try to change it! Don't say, "Oh, we were told we should not do this." No should, no shouldn't. Just observe what's going on.

* Then study those judgments. Observe what exactly they are and where they come from, strive to understand them, this time without any sermonizing or guilt or even any desire, much less effort to change them. Journal about what you discover.

NOTES TO MYSELF: _____

_____

_____

_____

_____

_____

_____

_____

_____

_____

_____

_____

_____

_____

_____

WEEK 21

Everyone at some time or the other experiences feelings of what is known as insecurity. You feel insecure about money, about the love of another, about your worth. Or you may be insecure regarding your health or your age or your physical appearance. If you were asked the question "What is it that makes me feel insecure?" you would almost certainly give the wrong answer. You would point to some external factor or condition, not realizing the source of insecurity is not outside of you but inside, caused by the programming society drilled into you, habitually producing insecure thoughts in your head. Insecurity all depends on the programming one receives. Thus, a person can feel secure with truly little money in the bank, while another is insecure with millions of dollars to spare. One person can be secure and trusting in a relationship, while another's insecurity makes them possessive and jealous. The difference is their programming. If, through awareness, you came to understand that it is believing insecure thoughts that causes you to doubt the invulnerability of your essential self, then your insecurity would vanish in a second, even though everything in the outside world remained exactly as it was before.

> If you were asked the question "What is it that makes me feel insecure?" you would almost certainly give the wrong answer.

If you wish to deal with your feelings of insecurity, there are four facts that you must study well and understand. First, it is futile to ease your insecure feelings by trying to change things outside of you. The relief that changing externals may bring will be short-lived. So, it is not worth the energy and time you spend in improving your physical appearance or making more money or getting an advanced degree or changing jobs.

Second, the above insight will lead you to tackle the problem where it really is: inside your head. Think of the people who, in exactly the same condition that you find yourself in now, would not feel the slightest insecurity. There are such people. Therefore, the problem lies not with reality outside of you but with you and the way you were programmed.

Third, you must understand that this programming of yours was picked up from insecure people who, when you were very young and impressionable, taught you by their behavior and their panic reactions that every time the outside world did not conform to a certain pattern, you must create an emotional turmoil within yourself called insecurity and then do everything in your power to rearrange the outside world—to make more money, seek more reassurances, condescend to authority, etc. This realization alone, that you don't have to do this to yourself, brings considerable relief.

Fourth, whenever you are insecure about what may happen in the future, just remember this: in the past you have been insecure about events which either didn't happen or you were able to handle somehow. Given this, you can let go of the future and enjoy the present moment, because life shows us we can only cope with things when they are present, not before they occur. The present always gives us the resources and the energy to deal with life. Set your mind on God's kingdom before everything else and all the rest will come to you as well.

Self-Observation

Said a world-famous violinist about his success in playing Beethoven's Violin Concerto: "I have splendid music, a splendid violin, and a splendid bow. All I need to do is bring them together and get out of the way."

From *Praying Naked*

THIS WEEK, FOCUS ON THE FOLLOWING:

* Be open and alert to identifying your insecurities. Start by making a list of your insecurities and adding to it as you detect others. Be aware of the self-condemnation and self-doubt they cause you. Journal about it.

* Once you have identified your insecurities, step back from them and study them. See who or what programmed them into you, and observe the critical voice in your head that they produce. Ask yourself why you believe that voice unquestioningly. Consider the ways your insecurity becomes self-fulfilling, how it thwarts your growth and self-worth—but only study it toward a better understanding of insecurity that can free you to be infinitely more loving toward yourself. Search inside yourself for the treasures buried under your insecurity, and as you allow them to surface, be sensitive to a mysteriously loving attitude arising effortlessly within you, moving out through you to every living creature. Journal about all this.

Notes to Myself: _____

_____

_____

_____

_____

_____

_____

_____

_____

_____

_____

_____

_____

_____

WEEK 22

The universe is made up of experiences that are designed to burn
out our reactivity, which is our attachment, our clinging, to pain, to
pleasure, to fear, to all of it. And as long as there are places where we're
vulnerable, the universe will find ways to confront us with them.

—Ram Dass

Do you want a sign that you're asleep? Here it is: you're suffering. If you're suffering, you're asleep. Suffering is a sign that you're out of touch with the truth. Suffering is given to you that you might open your eyes to the truth, that you might understand that there's falsehood somewhere, just as physical pain is given to you so you will understand that there is disease or illness somewhere. When your illusions clash with reality, when your falsehoods clash with truth, then you have suffering. Otherwise there is no suffering.

> "When your illusions clash with reality, when your falsehoods clash with truth, then you have suffering. Otherwise there is no suffering."

When you said, "I am a success," you were in error—and you were plunged into darkness. You identified yourself with success. The same thing is true when you said, "I am a failure," or when you ascribed any label to yourself. You know what's going to happen to you if you identify yourself with these things. You're going to cling to them, you're going to be worried that at any moment your world of things and people and ventures that you have put in place will slip out of your control and let you down, as it

129

often does. Yes, happy events do make life delightful, but they do not lead to self-discovery and growth and freedom. That privilege is reserved to the things and persons and situations that cause us pain. Suffering points out an area in you where you have not yet grown, where you need to grow and be transformed and changed. If you knew how to use that suffering, oh, how you would grow. The disappointment you experience when things don't turn out as you wanted them to—watch that! Look at what it says about you, without condemnation, otherwise you're going to get caught in self-hatred. Observe it as you would observe it in another person. Look at that disappointment, that depression you experience when you are criticized. What does that say about you? That worry, that anxiety, what does it say about you? Here is a simple truth of life that most people never discover: negative feelings, every negative feeling, is useful for awareness, for understanding, for growth. Every painful event contains in itself a seed of growth and liberation.

Self-Observation

The Jewish mystic Baal Shem had a curious way of praying to God. "Remember, Lord," he would say, "you need me just as much as I need you. If you did not exist, whom would I pray to? If I did not exist, who would do the praying?" It brought me so much joy to think that if I had not sinned, God would have no occasion to be forgiving.

From *The Song of the Bird*

THIS WEEK, FOCUS ON THE FOLLOWING:

✴ Recall some recent event that caused you anxiety, insecurity, jealousy, subjugation, whatever negative feelings that happen within you. Consider that whoever or whatever caused those feelings was your teacher because it revealed so much to you about yourself that you probably did not know, leading to greater self-understanding, self-discovery, and therefore growth and life and freedom. Journal about any insights this week that some form of suffering offered you.

* Then flip it. Explore times when you have caused pain and negative feelings in others and consider that at that moment you were a teacher to them, that your "happy fault" served as an instrument that planted a seed for self-discovery and growth in that person. Journal about this too.

NOTES TO MYSELF: _____

_____

_____

_____

_____

_____

_____

_____

_____

_____

_____

_____

_____

_____

_____

_____

_____

_____

_____

_____

_____

_____

_____

_____

_____

_____

_____

_____

_____

WEEK 23

A man said to a sage, "I want happiness." The sage said, "First remove 'me.' That's ego. Then," the sage added, "remove 'want.' That's desire. Now see how you are left with only happiness."

—Unknown

When you're ready to exchange your illusions for reality, when you're ready to exchange your dreams for facts, that's when life finally becomes meaningful. That's where life becomes beautiful. Can you imagine how liberating it is to never be disillusioned again, to never be disappointed again? You'll never feel let down again. Never feel rejected. Do you want to wake up? Do you want happiness? Do you want freedom? Here it is: drop your false ideas.

> Can you imagine how liberating it is to never be disillusioned again, to never be disappointed again? Never feel rejected. Do you want to wake up? Do you want happiness? Do you want freedom? Here it is: drop your false ideas.

* **The first false belief:** You cannot be happy without the people, outcomes, or things you are attached to, that you consider so precious. This is false. Again, there is not a single moment in your life when you do not have everything that you need to be happy. Think about that for a minute.

The reason you are unhappy is that you are focusing on what you do not have rather than on what you have right now.

* **The second false belief:** Happiness is in the future. Not true. Right here and now you are happy, and you do not know it because your false beliefs and your distorted perceptions have gotten you caught up in fears, anxieties, attachments, conflicts, guilt, and a host of games that you are programmed to play.

* **The third false belief:** Happiness will come if you manage to change the situation you are in and the people around you. It's not true. You foolishly squander so much energy trying to rearrange the world. If changing the world is your vocation in life, go right ahead and change it, but do not harbor the illusion that it will make you happy. If it is happiness that you seek, you can stop wasting your energy trying to get what you know cannot make you happy.

* **The fourth false belief:** If all your desires are fulfilled, you will finally be happy. Not true. In fact, it is these very desires and attachments that make you tense, frustrated, nervous, insecure, and fearful. Look at your list of your attachments and desires and to each of them, say these words: "Deep down in my heart, I know that even after I have gotten you, I will not get happiness." The fulfillment of desire can, at the most, bring flashes of pleasure and excitement. Don't mistake them for happiness.

We're striving to rearrange the world to attain and maintain the objects of our attachments under the false belief that it will bring us happiness. The good news is you can be happy right now, without people, things, and desired outcomes. You can love everyone without needing anyone. You can even be happy *with* your neurosis. You have everything you need to be happy right here, right now, with your life exactly as it is. The only reason you're not experiencing bliss at this present moment is because you're thinking or focusing on what you don't have, instead of what you have.

Self-Observation

The devil once went for a walk with a friend. They saw a man ahead of them stoop down and pick up something from the ground.

"What did that man find?" asked the friend.

"A piece of truth," said the devil.

"Doesn't that disturb you?" asked the friend.

"No," said the devil, "I shall let him make a belief out of it."

A religious belief is a signpost pointing the way to truth. When you cling to the signpost you are prevented from moving toward the truth because you think you have it already.

From *The Song of the Bird*

THIS WEEK, FOCUS ON THE FOLLOWING:

* Take time again to review your list of attachments you made in Week 6. To each person or thing listed there, say: "I am not really attached to this at all. I am merely deluding myself into the belief that without this person or thing or outcome I will not be happy."
* Reflect on the four false beliefs from this week and how they have thwarted your happiness. Do this honestly and see the change that comes about within you. Journal about it and how you have changed thus far in using this book.

Notes to Myself: _____

_____

_____

_____

_____

_____

_____

_____

_____

_____

_____

_____

_____

_____

PART 2

THE LAND OF LOVE

Love comes to the surface in your life signaling that it was there within you waiting to be released.

—Anthony De Mello

WEEK 24

The Kingdom of God is within you.

—Jesus Christ

God's kingdom is love. What does it mean to love? It means to be sensitive to life, to things, to persons, to feel for everything and everyone to the exclusion of nothing and no one. For exclusion can only be achieved through a hardening of oneself, through closing one's doors. And the moment there is a hardening, sensitivity dies. It won't be hard for you to find examples of this kind of sensitivity in your life.

> The moment you say so-and-so is cruel or defensive or even wise and loving, or whatever, you have hardened your perception and become prejudiced and ceased to perceive this person moment by moment.

Have you ever stopped to remove a stone or a nail from the road lest someone come to harm? It does not matter that you will never know the person who will benefit from this gesture and you will receive no reward or recognition. You just do it from a feeling of benevolence and kindness. Or have you felt pained at the wanton destruction in another part of the world, of a forest that you will never see and never benefit from? Have you gone to some trouble to help a stranger find his way though you do not know and will never meet this person again, purely from a good-heartedness that you feel within you? In these and so many

141

other moments, love comes to the surface in your life signaling that it was there within you waiting to be released.

How can you come to possess this kind of love? You cannot, because love is already there within you, but you can block its presence. As soon as a conclusion you have made about someone hardens into a belief about who they are, your attitude toward them becomes fixed and you are no longer capable of love's sensitivity. You are prejudiced and will see from the eye of that prejudice. In other words, you will cease to see this person again. If previously they behaved badly but then changed, you will not see them as they are now; you will only see the past. So how can you be sensitive to someone you do not even see? The moment you say so-and-so is cruel or defensive or even wise and loving, or whatever, you have hardened your perception and become prejudiced and ceased to perceive this person moment by moment, somewhat like a pilot who operates today with last week's weather report.

The mere realization that these are beliefs, conclusions, and prejudices, not reflections of reality, will cause them to drop.

Self-Observation

A young man became obsessed with a passion for Truth so he took leave of his family and friends and set out in search of it. He traveled over many lands, sailed across many oceans, climbed many mountains, and, all in all, went through a great deal of hardship and suffering.

One day he awoke to find he was seventy-five years old and had still not found the Truth he had been searching for. So he decided, sadly, to give up the search and go back home.

It took him months to return to his hometown, for he was an old man now. Once home, he opened the door of his house—and there he found Truth that had been patiently waiting for him all those years.

From *The Prayer of the Frog*

THIS WEEK, FOCUS ON THE FOLLOWING:

* Take two acquaintances, one you like and one you dislike, and on the basis of how you relate to each, list the many positive conclusions you have arrived at with the one you like and the many negative conclusions you have arrived at with the one you dislike. Journal about the ways in which these conclusions have hardened into beliefs about who each person is, blocking the sensitivity to see them without prejudice or any desire to judge them.
* Take a hard look at these beliefs and see how your view of these two people is fixed by your beliefs, conclusions, and prejudices that do not reflect reality. Notice how your sensitivity increases as you drop what you believed was true.

Notes to Myself: _____

_____

_____

_____

_____

_____

_____

_____

_____

_____

_____

_____

_____

_____

WEEK 25

This is my commandment, that you love one another
as I have loved you.

—Jesus Christ

What does one have to do to attain the quality of love Jesus demonstrated? Nothing! There is nothing you can do to attain it because you have it already. That is the first quality of love. Love is the very essence of your being. Anything you do to attain it will only make it forced, cultivated, and therefore phony, for love cannot be forced. However, love's presence can be blocked, but there is something you can do to remove the block. Observe the marvelous change that comes over you the moment you stop seeing people as good and bad, as saints and sinners, and begin to see them as unaware and ignorant. You must drop your false belief that people can sin in awareness. No one can sin in the light of awareness. Sin occurs not, as we mistakenly think, in malice, but in ignorance: "Father, forgive them, for they know not what they do."

> You must drop your false belief that people can sin in awareness. No one can sin in the light of awareness. Sin occurs not, as we mistakenly think, in malice, but in ignorance.

The second quality of love is its gratuitousness. Like the shade of the tree, the beauty of the rose, the light from the lamp, it gives and asks for nothing in return. Think of the man whose choice of wife is determined not by any quality she may have but by the amount of money she

147

will bring as dowry. Such a man, we rightly say, loves not the woman but the financial benefit she brings him. But is your own love any different when you seek the company of those who bring you emotional gratification and avoid those who don't; when you are positively disposed toward people who give you what you want and live up to your expectations and are negative or indifferent toward those who don't? Here, too, there is only one thing that you need to do to acquire this quality of gratuitousness that characterizes love. You can open your eyes and see. Just seeing, just exposing your so-called love for what it really is—a camouflage for selfishness and greed—is a major step toward arriving at this second quality of love.

The third quality of love is its unselfconsciousness. Love so enjoys the loving that it is blissfully unaware of itself. The way the lamp is busy shining with no thought of whether it is benefiting others or not. The way a rose gives out its fragrance simply because there is nothing else it can do, whether there is someone to enjoy the fragrance or not. The way the tree offers its shade. The light, the fragrance, and the shade are not produced at the approach of persons and turned off when there is no one there. These things, like love, exist independently of persons. Love simply is; it has no object. The benefit it bestows simply is present, regardless of whether someone will benefit from it or not. So, the tree, the rose, and the lamp have no consciousness of any merit or of doing good. When the giving is pure, the left hand has no consciousness of what the right hand does.

The final quality of love is its freedom. The moment coercion or control or conflict enters, love dies. Think how the rose, the tree, the lamp leave you completely free. The tree will make no effort to drag you into its shade if you are in danger of sunstroke. The rose will not try to awaken you to beauty as you walk mindlessly down the lane. The lamp will not force its light on you lest you stumble in the dark. And yet it is forever there, yours for the taking.

Self-Observation

"Prisoner at the bar," said the Grand Inquisitor, "you are charged with encouraging people to break the laws, traditions, and customs of our holy religion. How do you plead?"

"Guilty, Your Honor."

"And with frequenting the company of heretics, prostitutes, public sinners, the extortionist tax-collectors, the colonial conquerors of our nation—in short, the excommunicated. How do you plead?"

"Guilty, Your Honor."

"Finally, you are charged with revising, correcting, calling into question the sacred tenets of our faith. How do you plead?"

"Guilty, Your Honor."

"What is your name, prisoner?"

"Jesus Christ, Your Honor."

From *The Prayer of the Frog*

THIS WEEK, FOCUS ON THE FOLLOWING:

* Think of someone you judge as no-good, or as sinful, or as mean or greedy or crooked, whatever. In short, someone whose behavior you think warrants condemnation and exclusion. Journal about the reasons you believe your judgment is justified.

* Next, try seeing some glimmer of light shining through this person and consider the possibility that their bad behavior stems not from malice, but ignorance. Journal how this might change the way you would relate to this person. Contemplate this. Contemplation alone can cause all your judgments to drop. The moment the

heavy weight of your judgments drop, freedom will arise, which is just another word for love. Journal about this too.

NOTES TO MYSELF: _____

_____

_____

_____

_____

_____

_____

_____

_____

_____

_____

_____

_____

_____

WEEK 26

Love does not cause suffering: what causes it is the sense of ownership,
which is love's opposite.

—Antoine de Saint-Exupéry

The biggest enemy of love is desire. You know why? Because if I desire you, I want to possess you. I can't leave you free for fear of losing you. That's not love; not perfect love. There's no fear in perfect love. You know why? Because there's no desire. Where there is love, there is no desire. I mean desire in the sense of attachment. But you've been programmed to believe that attachment is love. That's how stupid our culture is. Anyone expecting to find life here will find only death and misery. I run into people of all kinds, religious and nonreligious people, atheists, laypeople, priests and sisters and bishops. Rarely do I find someone who knows what love is. Most are operating on the wrong instructions.

Attachment means, "I must have you." It means, "By damn, I'll do everything to manipulate you into wanting me because without you I cannot be happy." And it means that after I finally make you my own, I'll demand you meet my conditions for loving you or I'll withdraw my love until you do. It's in all the love songs, all the advertisements, and all the poems and greeting cards. There, you've got the formula for divorce. There, you've got the formula for quarrels. There, you've got the formula for relationships falling apart.

A full-blown attachment comes with an insensitivity to anything that isn't part of your attachment. Each time you cling to the object of your attachment, you leave your heart there, so you cannot invest it in the next place you go to, the next person you are with. The symphony of life moves on but you keep looking back, clinging to a few bars of the melody, blocking your ears to the rest of the music, thereby producing disharmony and conflict between what life is offering you and what you are clinging to. Then comes the tension and anxiety which are the very death of love and the joyful freedom that love brings. For love and freedom are only found when one enjoys each note as it arises, then allows it to go, so as to be fully receptive to the notes that follow.

Love means, "I'm perfectly happy without you, darling, it's all right." It means, "I wish you nothing but good, and I leave you free. If we truly connect, I'm delighted; and when we don't, I'm not miserable. When you go away, I don't miss you. I don't feel pain, because where there is sorrow, there is no love."

> "A full-blown attachment comes with an insensitivity to anything that isn't part of your attachment. Each time you cling to the object of your attachment, you leave your heart there, so you cannot invest it in . . . the next person you are with."

Self-Observation

When Buddha entered the capital of King Prasanjit, the king in person came out to him. He had been a friend of Buddha's father and had heard of the lad's renunciation. So he attempted to persuade Buddha to give up his life as a wandering beggar and return to the palace, thinking he was doing a service to his old friend.

Buddha looked into the eyes of Prasanjit and said, "Answer me truthfully. For all your outer merriment, has your kingdom brought you a single day of happiness?"

Prasanjit lowered his eyes and was silent.

From *The Heart of the Enlightened*

THIS WEEK, FOCUS ON THE FOLLOWING:

* Journal about a person to whom you are strongly attached and without whom you believe you cannot be happy.
* Now imagine saying to this person, "I'm perfectly happy without you, darling. I wish you nothing but good, and I leave you free. When we truly connect, I'm delighted; and when we don't, I'm not miserable. When you go away, I don't miss you." Journal about your experience in relating to a loved one in this way. Does it cause a shock? Journal about it. Does it liberate you in some way? Journal about this too.

Notes to Myself: _____

_____

_____

_____

_____

_____

_____

_____

_____

_____

_____

_____

_____

WEEK 27

Children begin by loving their parents. After a time they judge them.
Rarely, if ever, do they forgive them.

—Oscar Wilde

I have said that it's not the people around us who have upset us, and that it's not ourselves, but it's our programming. And so you may ask, is it not the people who were around us who have programmed us when we were young?

Yes, they did. But they didn't set out with any malice to do this to us. They're the victims of what other people have done to them.

Again and again, people come to me who are so upset about their parents. They can't forgive their parents; they hate their parents. All right, I understand. I'm not saying that your parents did right or they did wrong. Maybe they did wrong. But look, could you understand them? Because that's what love is all about. Love is not blaming others. Love is not judging others.

> **The Chinese have a saying that when the eye is unobstructed, the result is sight. When the ear is unobstructed, the result is hearing. And when the heart is unobstructed, the result is joy and love.**

Love is not condemning others. Love is understanding. Can you see that? The Chinese have a saying that when the eye is unobstructed, the result is sight. When the ear is unobstructed, the result is hearing. And when the heart is unobstructed, the result is joy and love. It is a sobering thought that the finest act of love you can perform is not an act of service but an act of contemplation, of seeing. When you see people in their inner beauty and goodness you transform and create.

Can you understand how there's so much goodwill in your parents, and so much helplessness, and so much programming, and so much confusion, and so much fear? Have you ever paused to understand this?

If you were to do this, your attitude would change into love and forgiveness, and you would discover to your joy that you are being transformed by this strangely loving attitude that arises within you and moves out through you to every living creature.

Self-Observation

A beggar saw a banker coming out of his office and said, "Could you give me a dime, sir, for a cup of coffee?"

The banker felt sorry for this man, who looked bedraggled and distraught. He said, "Here's a dollar. Take it and have ten cups of coffee."

The next day the beggar was there again at the steps of the banker's office and as the banker came out he punched him.

"Hey," said the banker. "What are you doing?"

"You and your lousy ten cups of coffee. They kept me awake the whole of last night!"

From *The Heart of the Enlightened*

This week, focus on the following:

* Journal about a grievance that you still have with one or both of your parents and haven't yet forgiven. Get in touch with the pain this causes you.

* Can you understand your parents' ignorance and where it came from? Can you understand how there may have been so little malice there, and so much ignorance? Can you understand how there may have been so much goodwill, and yet so much helplessness, and so much confusion and fear in your parents? Journal about all this.

NOTES TO MYSELF: _____

_____

_____

_____

_____

_____

_____

_____

_____

_____

_____

_____

_____

_____

WEEK 28

He who takes offense when no offense is intended is a fool,
and he who takes offense when offense is intended is a greater fool.

—Brigham Young

You've got people you're living with and you're having difficulty in these relationships. Human relations are never difficult; it's your programming that's difficult. There are never any difficulties in relating to people, only difficulties in your programming. How come you're getting upset? How come when anyone pulls a little string, you jump? You ask, "Is it possible to live with someone who's losing his temper every day and for me not to get upset?" Yes, very much so. You ask, "When somebody insults you, is it possible not to get upset?" Yes, that's right. It's a simple as a letter arrives and you send it back to that person marked "Return to sender." You don't even open it; you send it back. You know why you got insulted or why you were upset by the insult? Because you took it, that's why. Silly, why did you take it? "You mean that it's possible not to take it?" Yes! It becomes irrelevant to you.

Do you know what it means to be human? It's something like this: A guy buys a newspaper every day from a newspaper vendor. The newspaper vendor is always rude to him. So a friend of his says, "Why do you buy your paper from this guy? He's always rude to you. Why don't you buy it from the vendor next door?" This guy answers, "Why should the vendor decide where I buy my newspaper? Why should he have the power to decide that for me?" Now you're talking about a human being. Otherwise, you're talking about monkeys you can control and get to act in predictable ways by a little twist of their tail. It's programming. Programming!

So, it isn't the person who's upset you. It isn't you who have upset yourself. It's your programming. All you have to do is understand this and distance yourself from it and the thing will take care of itself, it really will.

As Lao Tzu said, "If you correct your mind, the rest of your life will fall into place."

> You'll be amazed how in only a few months of practicing the simple steps of awareness, things that before would have made you sick with anxiety, or with suffering, or with whatever, you can take in your stride with perfect peace.

You'll be amazed how in only a few months of practicing the simple steps of awareness, things that before would have made you sick with anxiety, or with suffering, or with whatever, you can take in your stride with perfect peace. You understand where it is coming from. You're quite relaxed about it. That's the spiritual life. That's dying to yourself—dropping that programming. Understanding it for what it is is how it drops.

❁

Self-Observation

Buddha seemed quite unruffled by the insults hurled at him by a visitor. When his disciples later asked him what the secret of his serenity was, he said:

"Imagine what would happen if someone placed an offering before you and you did not pick it up. Or someone sent you a letter that you refused to open; you would be unaffected by its contents, would you not? Do this each time you are abused and you will not lose your serenity."

From *The Prayer of the Frog*

THIS WEEK, FOCUS ON THE FOLLOWING:

* Recall an incident when someone insulted you and the feeling of loneliness that followed being insulted.
* Now look at the insult again. Imagine this time you see the insult as external to you and having nothing to do with you, that it isn't really the person who has upset you, nor is it you who have upset yourself. It's your programming. Can you see in your reaction your programmed attachment to acceptance and approval, to being appreciated and applauded? Can you see how this attachment involves never-ending tension in certain if not all of your relationships? Understand this as true and then distance yourself from the insult. That is all that is needed for your upset to drop, along with your attachment to approval. Journal about this.

Notes to Myself: _____

_____

_____

_____

_____

_____

_____

_____

_____

_____

_____

_____

_____

_____

WEEK 29

Everything you behold without is a judgment of
what you beheld within.

—A Course in Miracles

Think of someone you dislike, someone you generally avoid because his or her presence generates negative feelings in you. Imagine yourself in this person's presence now and watch the negative emotions arise and consider for a moment that you are quite conceivably in the presence of someone who is deprived, crippled, and blind.

Now understand that if you invite this person, this beggar from the streets and alleys, into your home, that is, into your presence, he or she will make you a gift that none of your charming, pleasant friends can make you, rich as they are. This poor person is going to reveal yourself to you and reveal human nature to you, a revelation as precious as any found in Scripture, for what will it profit you to know all the Scriptures if you do not know yourself and so live the life of a robot? The revelation that this beggar is going to bring will widen your heart till there is room in it for every living creature.

Can there be a finer gift than that?

This poor person here in front of you is crippled and blind and lame, not stubborn and malicious as you so foolishly thought. Understand this truth; look at it steadfastly and deeply, and you will see your negative emotions soften and gradually turn into gentleness and compassion. Suddenly you have room in your heart for someone who was consigned to the streets and alleys by others and by you.

Now you will realize that this beggar came to your home with alms for you—the widening of your heart in compassion and the release of your spirit

171

in freedom. Where before you used to be controlled by these persons—they had the power to create negative emotions in you and you went out of your way to avoid them—now you have the gift of freedom to avoid no one, to go anywhere.

> "Where before you used to be controlled by these persons—they had the power to create negative emotions in you and you went out of your way to avoid them—now you have the gift of freedom to avoid no one, to go anywhere."

When you see this, you will notice how the feeling of compassion in your heart has been added to the feeling of gratitude for this beggar who is your benefactor. And another new, unaccustomed feeling: you feel a desire to seek out the company of these growth-producing crippled, blind, and lame people, the way someone who has learned to swim seeks water, because each time you are with them, where before you used to feel the oppression and tyranny of negative feelings, you can now actually feel an ever-expanding compassion and the freedom of the skies. And you can barely recognize yourself as you see yourself going out into the streets and alleys of the town, in obedience to the master's injunction, to bring in the poor, the crippled, the blind, and the lame.

Self-Observation

One day Abraham invited a beggar to his tent for a meal. When grace was being said the man began to curse God, declaring he could not bear to hear His name. Seized with indignation, Abraham drove the blasphemer away. When he was at his prayers that night, God said to him, "This man has cursed and reviled me for fifty years and yet I have given him food to eat every day. Could you not put up with him for a single meal?"

From *The Prayer of the Frog*

THIS WEEK, FOCUS ON THE FOLLOWING:

* Take another look at this person you dislike and avoid, and ask yourself the following question: "Am I in charge of this situation or is it in charge of me?" That is the first revelation. With it comes the second: the way to be in charge of this situation is to be in charge of yourself, which you are not. How do you achieve this mastery? Understand that there are people who, if they were in your place, would not be negatively affected by this person. They would be in charge of the situation, not subject to it. Therefore, your negative feelings are caused not by this person as you mistakenly think but by your programming.

* Here is the third and major revelation. Consider that this behavior, this trait in the other person that seemed to cause you to react negatively, was not their fault. They were not responsible for it; it was their programming. Consider that you can hold on to your negative feelings only when you mistakenly believe that he or she is free and aware and therefore responsible for their malice. To be malevolent is not freedom but a sickness, for it implies a lack of consciousness and sensitivity. Can you see this? See what happens when you really understand this. Journal about it.

NOTES TO MYSELF: _____

_____

_____

_____

_____

_____

_____

_____

_____

_____

_____

_____

_____

_____

WEEK 29

175

WEEK 30

It is in giving that we receive.

—St. Francis of Assisi

There are three types of selfishness. The first type is the one where I give myself the pleasure of pleasing myself. That's what we generally call self-centeredness. The second is when I give myself the pleasure of pleasing others. That would be a more refined kind of selfishness. The first one is very obvious, but the second one is hidden, very hidden, and for that reason more dangerous, because we get to feel that we're really great. But maybe we're not all that great after all.

So, by example, imagine someone who lives alone and goes to a charitable organization to volunteer several hours of their time. Can you see they're really doing it for a selfish reason—they need a way that makes them feel like they're contributing to the world. So, charity can be seen as a kind of two-way street of giving and receiving. In other words, giving and receiving are the same thing. If you can see that, you're almost enlightened! "I give something, I get something." That's beautiful. That's true. That's real. That isn't charity, that's enlightened self-interest.

> "... ordinarily everything we do is in our self-interest. Everything. When you do something for the love of Christ, is that selfishness? Yes. When you're doing something for the love of anybody, it is in your self-interest."

You might object to this, but I'm not saying there's no such thing as pure motivation. I'm saying that ordinarily everything we do is in our *self-interest*. Everything. When you do something for the love of Christ, is that selfishness? Yes. When you're doing something for the love of anybody, it is in your self-interest. Suppose you happen to live in a big city and you feed over five hundred children a day. That would give you a good feeling, right? You wouldn't expect it to give you a bad feeling, but sometimes it does. And that is because there are some people who do things so that they won't have to have a bad feeling, and they call *that* charity. Some are acting out of guilt. That isn't love, but thank God you do things for people and thank God it's pleasurable. Wonderful! That's healthy. You are a healthy individual because you are *self-interested*. What I am saying is that when you do something of the first type of selfishness, giving yourself the pleasure of pleasing yourself, or when you do something of the second type of selfishness, giving yourself the pleasure of pleasing others, don't take pride in that. Don't think you're a great person. You're getting your pleasure all the same.

There is the third type of selfishness, which is the worst. It involves doing something good so that you won't suffer a bad feeling. With this type, doing good doesn't give you a good feeling; rather doing it gives you a bad feeling. You may even hate it. You're making loving sacrifices but you're grumbling all the while. Do you think you don't do good things that way? Ha! I certainly have. You know how it goes. "Could I meet you tonight, Father De Mello?" "Yes, come on in!" I say, but I don't want to meet with him; I hate meeting with him. I want to watch that TV show tonight, but how do I say no to him? I don't have the guts to say no. So I put on a smile and say, "Come on in," and I put on a smile but the whole time I'm silently complaining, thinking I am going to be happy when this thing is over. That's the worst kind of charity, when you don't have the guts to say "no" because you don't want a bad feeling. Because you want people to think you're good and to like you for it.

Self-Observation

A farmer, whose corn always took the first prize at the state fair, had the habit of sharing his best corn seed with all the farmers in the neighborhood.

When asked why, he said, "It is really a matter of self-interest. The wind picks up the pollen and carries it from field to field. So if my neighbors grow inferior corn, the cross-pollination brings down the quality of my own corn. That is why I am concerned that they plant only the very best."

From *The Prayer of the Frog*

THIS WEEK, FOCUS ON THE FOLLOWING:

* Think of the last time you gave yourself to yourself. Then think about the last time you gave to someone else. Can you see that both are really about the same thing, namely about you pleasing you? Reflect on the principle that giving and receiving are the same and journal about what that means to you.

* Next, think about a sacrifice you made in giving your time or money or assistance to another when you really didn't want to but went ahead and gave anyway. Was it because you didn't want to feel guilty or because you wanted others to see you as good and admire you for it? Journal about this.

NOTES TO MYSELF: _____

_____

_____

_____

_____

_____

_____

_____

_____

_____

_____

_____

_____

WEEK 30

WEEK 31

If you expect nothing from somebody, you are never disappointed.

—Sylvia Plath

A young man came to complain that his girlfriend had let him down, that she had played false. What are you complaining about? Did you expect any better? Expect the worst; you're dealing with selfish people. You're the idiot—you glorified her, didn't you? You thought she was a princess, you thought people were nice. They're not! They're not nice. They're as bad as you are—bad, you understand? They're asleep like you. And what do you think they are going to seek? Their own self-interest, exactly like you. No difference.

> You are never in love with anyone. You're only in love with your prejudiced and hopeful idea of that person. Take a minute to think about that.

Do you think you help people because you are in love with them? Well, I've got news for you. You are never in love with anyone. You're only in love with your prejudiced and hopeful idea of that person. Take a minute to think about that: you are never in love with anyone, you're in love with your prejudiced idea of that person.

Isn't that how you fall out of love? Your idea changes, doesn't it? "How could you let me down when I trusted you so much?" you say to someone. Did you really trust them? You never trusted anyone. Come off it! That's part of society's brainwashing. You never trust anyone. You only trust your judgment about that person. So what are you complaining about?

The fact is that you don't like to say, "My judgment was lousy." That's not very flattering to you, is it? So you prefer to say, "How could you have let me down?"

So there it is: people don't really want to grow up, people don't really want to change, people don't really want to be happy. We want to depend on others psychologically—to depend on others emotionally. What does that imply? It means to depend on another human being for my happiness. Think about that. Because when you do, the next thing you will be doing, whether you're aware of it or not, is demanding that other people contribute to your happiness. Then the next step will be fear—fear of loss, fear of alienation, fear of rejection, mutual control.

It is said that perfect love casts out fear. And where there is love there are no demands, no expectations, no dependency. I do not demand that you make me happy; my happiness does not lie in you. If you were to leave me, I will not feel sorry for myself. I enjoy your company immensely, but I do not cling to you.

Self-Observation

A mother asks her son, "What does your girlfriend like in you?"
"She thinks I'm handsome, talented, clever, and a good dancer."
"And what do you like about her?"
"She thinks I'm handsome, talented, clever, and a good dancer."

From *The Prayer of the Frog*

THIS WEEK, FOCUS ON THE FOLLOWING:

* Think of a time when you were heartbroken and thought you would never be happy again. What happened? Did time go on and

did you manage to pick up another attachment, to find somebody else you were attracted to? If so, what happened to the old attachment? Journal about it.

* Now imagine how liberating it would be for you not to depend emotionally on anyone. Think of someone you love. Imagine saying to this person, "I'd rather have my freedom than your love and I am willing to leave you free to be yourself." The moment you say that you will observe one of two things: either your heart will resist those words and you will be exposed for the clinger and exploiter that we all are; or your heart will pronounce the words sincerely and in that very instant all control, manipulation, exploitation, possessiveness, jealousy, specialness will drop. Which one of these two do you observe in you? Journal about it.

NOTES TO MYSELF: _____

_____

_____

_____

_____

_____

_____

_____

_____

_____

_____

_____

_____

WEEK 32

In a society that says, "Put yourself last," self-love and
self-acceptance are almost revolutionary.

—Brené Brown

When your mother got angry with you, she didn't say there was something wrong with her, she said there was something wrong with you; otherwise she wouldn't have been angry. Well, I made the great discovery that if you are angry, it's not mine. There's something wrong with you. So you'd better cope with your anger. Stay with it and cope with it. Spirituality is awareness, awareness, awareness, awareness, awareness, awareness. Whether there's something wrong with me or not, I'll examine that independently of your anger. I'm not going to be influenced by your anger. If you slam a book on the table in disgust, I'm not going to pick up the book for you. I'm not going to rescue you or soothe you and tell you it's all right.

> When we talk about self-worth, are we not talking, really, about how we are reflected in the mirrors of other people's minds or behaviors? We don't need to depend on that.

The funny thing is that when I can do this without feeling any negativity toward another, I can be quite objective about myself too. Only a very aware person can refuse to pick up the guilt and anger and can say, "You're having a tantrum. Too bad. I don't feel the slightest desire to rescue you anymore, and I refuse to feel guilty. I'm not going to hate myself for anything I've done." That's what guilt is. I'm not going to give myself a bad feeling and whip myself for anything I have done, either right or wrong. I'm ready to analyze it, to watch it, and say, "Well, if I did wrong, it was in unawareness."

When we talk about self-worth, are we not talking, really, about how we are reflected in the mirrors of other people's minds or behaviors? We don't need to depend on that. One understands one's personal worth when one no longer identifies or defines oneself in terms of these things. I'm not beautiful or ugly because society says I am. I'm not worthy or unworthy because society accepts or rejects me. There is a quality of being, a presence that is above all this, watching what comes and goes nonjudgmentally, unaffected by any of it.

Self-Observation

The Zen master Ryokan lived a very simple life in a little hut at the foot of the mountain.

One night, when the master was away, a thief broke into the hut only to discover that there was nothing to steal.

Ryokan returned and caught the burglar. "You have put yourself to much trouble to visit me," he said. "You must not go away empty-handed. Please take my clothes and blanket as a gift."

The thief, quite bewildered, took the clothes and slunk off.

Ryokan sat down naked and watched the moon. "Poor fellow," he thought to himself, "I wish I could give him the gorgeous moonlight."

From *The Song of the Bird*

THIS WEEK, FOCUS ON THE FOLLOWING:

* Each day this week, take a break from the world and do this simple exercise. Be aware of your presence in the room where you are. Simply say to yourself, "I'm in this room." Look at yourself as if from the outside. Notice a slightly different feeling than if you were looking at things in the room. Ask, "What is this beingness I am that is looking at me?"

* Keep reviewing this chapter this week and contemplate what it means to you to be in the world but not of it.

NOTES TO MYSELF: _____

_____

_____

_____

_____

_____

_____

_____

_____

_____

_____

_____

_____

WEEK 33

Be a ray of sunshine to everyone you meet.

—Rhonda Byrne

It is commonly held that only when you feel deeply loved are you able to go out in love to others. This is not true. A person in love does indeed go out to the world—not in love but in euphoria. For this person, the world takes on an unreal, rosy hue, which it loses the moment the euphoria dies. The so-called love is generated not by a clear perception of reality but by the conviction, true or false, that he or she is loved by someone. It is a conviction that is dangerously fragile because it is founded on the unreliable, changeable people who you believe love you and who can, at any moment, pull the switch and turn off this euphoria. No wonder those who walk this path never really lose their insecurity. Someone else controls the switch, and, when it is switched off, the glow fades away.

Left to its own devices, life would never produce love. Left to its own devices, life would only lead you to attraction, from attraction to pleasure, then to attachment, to satisfaction, which would finally lead to wearisomeness and boredom. After that would come a plateau. Then once again, the weary cycle: attraction, pleasure, attachment, fulfillment, satisfaction, boredom. All of this mixed with the anxieties, the jealousies, the possessiveness, the sorrow, and the pain that make the cycle a roller coaster.

When you have repeatedly gone around and around the cycle, a time finally comes when you have had enough and want to call a halt to the whole process. And if you are lucky enough not to run into something or someone else that catches your eye, you will have at least attained a fragile peace.

What does it mean to love? It means to see a person, a thing, a situation as it really is and not as you imagine it to be, and to give it the response it deserves. You cannot love what you do not even see. You cannot love what you cannot see afresh. You cannot love what you are not constantly discovering anew.

And what prevents you from seeing? Your concepts, your categories, your prejudices and projections, your needs and attachments, the labels you have drawn from your conditioning and from your past experiences. To see each person and thing anew in present-moment freshness is the most arduous thing a human being can undertake. For it calls for a disciplined, alert mind, whereas most people would much rather lapse into mental laziness. As I've stated before, the finest act of love you can perform is an act of contemplation, of seeing. When you see a person in their inner beauty and goodness, you offer an infinitely more loving gift than you can offer them through any act of service. For you have transformed them; you have created them in your heart and it will extend outwardly into reality. Moreover, to your joy you will discover that you are also being transformed by this strangely loving attitude that arises within you toward this thing you call yourself—an attitude that arises within you and moves out through you to every living creature.

> "Left to its own devices, life would never produce love. Left to its own devices, life would only lead you to attraction, from attraction to pleasure, then to attachment, to satisfaction, which would finally lead to wearisomeness and boredom."

Self-Observation

A Tale from Attar of Nishapur:

The lover knocked at the door of his beloved.

"Who knocks?" said the beloved from within.

"It is I," said the lover.

"Go away. This house will not hold you and me both."

The rejected lover went away into the desert. There he meditated for months on end, pondering the words of the beloved. Finally he returned and knocked at the door again.

"Who knocks?"

"It is you."

The door was immediately opened.

From *The Song of the Bird*

THIS WEEK, FOCUS ON THE FOLLOWING:

* Think of a person you like; someone whom you are drawn to and who is drawn to you. Now attempt to look at this person as if you were seeing them for the first time, not allowing yourself to be influenced by your past knowledge or experience of them. Look for things in them that you may have missed because of familiarity, for familiarity breeds staleness, blindness, and boredom.

* Now shift focus to a person you dislike. Search for the treasures buried in this person that your dislike prevented you from seeing before. As you do this, observe any change of attitude or feeling

that comes over you, as your dislike that clouded you from seeing drops away. Journal about this.

* Now, make this same gift to yourself. If you have been able to do it for another, this should be fairly easy. Follow the same procedure: no defect, no neurosis is judged or condemned. You have not judged others; you will be amazed now that you yourself are not being judged. Probe, study, and analyze those defects for a better understanding that leads to love and forgiveness. Journal about this.

WEEK 33

NOTES TO MYSELF: _____

_____

_____

_____

_____

_____

_____

_____

_____

_____

_____

_____

_____

199

WEEK 34

You will know love when the mind is very still and free from its
search for gratification and escapes.

—Jiddu Krishnamurti

Listen to the love songs on the radio. That's our culture's idea of love, but it isn't love at all, it's the opposite of love. It's desire and control and possessiveness. It's manipulation and fear and anxiety. Where there is love, there is no desire, but our culture cannot make any sense out of that statement. By desire I mean in the sense of attachment, but our culture's programming has us thinking, *Attachment is love*. It has you expecting to find love there. It has you expecting love to last there. But all you can find in attachment is conflict and misery. That's how stupid our culture can be. Love is such a simple, such a sublime, such an extraordinary thing, but I rarely run into someone who knows what love is. They all got the wrong instructions. If you're having any trouble with love—in your marriage or your family or a friendship—I'm going to give you something to think about. Has it ever occurred to you that what you call love is really your chain? For example, are you calling somebody your happiness, as in, "You are my joy, without you I'm lost, without you I'm nothing"? I invite you to ask yourself, "In whom do I seek my happiness?"

> " Love is such a simple, such a sublime, such an extraordinary thing, but I rarely run into someone who knows what love is. They all got the wrong instructions. "

Now reflect on this: whatever your answer, that's your prison. I know, this is hard language, but I invite you to look at it squarely—cut it, scrape it, melt it down, as the Buddha said—until you can see how you are imprisoned by your wrong ideas about love. But at the same time be clear: it's not because there's anything wrong with you. You're OK, you're great. We all are; there's nothing wrong with us. The essence of our being is love. It is our culture that put wrong ideas about love into our heads. We needn't spend too much time trying to catch the culprit; we just need to understand that we were taught to become attached, equating love with desires so intense that we would refuse to be happy unless our desires were fulfilled. Attachment is the enemy of love. Attachment is what causes the mess in our relationships. You know why? Because if I desire you, I want to possess you, so I've got to seduce you into desiring me. That's not love; that's conquest that, after the conquest, turns into possessiveness and jealousy.

Attachment means if I get you, I can't leave you free. I have to control you, insisting you measure up to the list of things I need you to become for me to be happy. Are you following what I'm saying? That's no love; that's fear. There's no fear in perfect love. You know why? Because there's no desire. If you would only sit down for two minutes and just watch how untrue your assumptions about love are, how much they are based on fear, you would be released from the fear that blocks love's presence. When the heart is unobstructed, the result is joy and love. Love means to leave everyone free and to be free yourself, to be special to no one and love everyone—because that is love. Love is inclusive. It shines on good and bad alike; it makes rain fall on saints and sinners alike. Is it possible for the rose to say, "I will give my fragrance to the good people but withhold it from the bad"? Is it possible for the lamp to say, "I will give my light to the good and withhold it from the bad"? Or for the tree to say, "I'll give my shade only to the good"? These are images of what love is about. It's been there all along, staring us in the face in the Scriptures, though we never cared to see it because we were so drowned in what our culture calls love.

Self-Observation

Every day in the corner of a library in Japan, an old monk was to be found sitting in peaceful meditation.

"I never see you read the sutras," said the librarian.

"I never learned to read," replied the monk.

"That's a disgrace. A monk like you ought to be able to read. Shall I help you?"

"Yes. Tell me," said the monk, pointing to himself, "What is the meaning of this character?"

Why light a torch when the sun shines in the heavens? Why water the ground when the rain pours down in torrents?

From *The Prayer of the Frog*

THIS WEEK, FOCUS ON THE FOLLOWING:

* Who are you calling your happiness, as in, "You are my joy, without you I'm lost, without you I'm nothing"? Again ask yourself, "In whom do I seek my happiness?"
* Reflect on the ways you have made this relationship a prison. Look at this squarely, how you are imprisoned by your wrong ideas about love that society put in your head. Journal about this.

Notes to Myself: _____

_____

_____

_____

_____

_____

_____

_____

_____

_____

_____

_____

_____

WEEK 35

Compassion is the radicalism of our time.

—Dalai Lama

The heart in love remains soft and sensitive. But when you're hell-bent on getting this or the other thing, you become ruthless, hard, and insensitive. How can you love people when you need people? You can only use them. If I need you to make me happy, I've got to use you, I've got to manipulate you, I've got to find ways and means of winning you. I cannot let you be free.

I can only love people when I have emptied my life of people. When I die to the need for people, then I'm right in the desert. In the beginning it feels awful, it feels lonely, but if you can take it for a while, you'll suddenly discover that it isn't lonely at all. It is solitude, it is aloneness, and the desert begins to flower.

Then at last you'll know what love is, what God is, what reality is. But in the beginning giving up the drug can be tough unless you have a very keen understanding or unless you have suffered enough. It's a great thing to have suffered. Only then can you get sick of it. You can make use of suffering to end suffering. But most people simply go on suffering. That explains the conflict I sometimes have between the role of spiritual director and that of therapist. A therapist says, "Let's ease the suffering." The spiritual director says, "Let her suffer, she'll get sick of this way of relating to people and she'll finally decide to break out of this prison of emotional dependence on others." This doesn't mean that when someone comes to me and is quite upset—let's say she is a victim of crime, or someone's mother has died—that I take the attitude of, "So, the fact that you're grieving, that you're upset, it means there's something wrong with you." Of course not. I extend understanding. Even if I see the grief comes from an attachment, I recognize that this person isn't causing it. I am compassionate with that person; I am understanding toward that person. And gently, when the person is ready, I can explain where their upset is coming from. Because ultimately, I am not being compassionate if I don't help them see through the pain to its real cause, meaning the way they have been programmed to become upset and afraid. If you come to me and you are very upset because someone has injured you, I'll be understanding of where you are coming from, I'll be compassionate toward you. But someday, sometime, somewhere, if you're ready, I'll slip you the secret that you don't have to suffer this way. I will point to another way that allows you to see through the pain to its cause, which is your programming. That to me would be true compassion.

> When I die to the need for people, then I'm right in the desert. In the beginning it feels awful, it feels lonely, but if you can take it for a while, you'll suddenly discover that it isn't lonely at all. It is solitude, it is aloneness, and the desert begins to flower.

We're always bothered by the tragic. Life is a mystery, which means your thinking mind cannot make sense out of it. For that you've got to wake up and then you'll suddenly realize that reality is not problematic, your programmed reaction to it is the problem. In the *Bhagavad Gita*, the Lord Krishna says to Arjuna, "Plunge into the heat of battle and keep your heart at the lotus feet of the Lord." As you use the sword of awareness to move from attachment into love, there is one thing you must keep in mind: don't be harsh or impatient, or hating of yourself or anyone else. How can love grow out of such attitudes? But rather hold on to the compassion and the matter-of-factness with which the surgeon plies his knife.

Self-Observation

The story goes that a fire broke out in a house in which a man was fast asleep. They tried to carry him out through the window. No way. They tried to carry him out through the door. No way. He was just too huge and heavy.

They were pretty desperate till someone suggested: "Wake him up, and then he'll get out by himself."

From *The Prayer of the Frog*

THIS WEEK, FOCUS ON THE FOLLOWING:

* Journal on what it means that you can only love people when you have emptied your life of people, when you die to the need for people.
* Journal about what it means that you are not being compassionate if you don't help someone struggling to see through the pain to its real cause, meaning the way they have been programmed to become upset and afraid.

NOTES TO MYSELF: _____

_____

_____

_____

_____

_____

_____

_____

_____

_____

_____

_____

_____

_____

_____

_____

_____

_____

_____

_____

_____

_____

_____

_____

_____

_____

_____

PART 3

REDISCOVERING LIFE

Life is for the gambler. The coward dies.

—**Anthony De Mello**

WEEK 36

It took me four years to paint like Raphael,
but a lifetime to paint like a child.

—Pablo Picasso

Jesus said, "Truly, I say to you, unless you turn and become like children, you will never enter the kingdom of heaven." The first quality that strikes one when one looks into the eyes of a child is their innocence: their lovely inability to lie or wear a mask or pretend to be anything other than what they is. A child is exactly like the rest of Nature. A dog is a dog; a rose, a rose; a star, a star; everything is quite simply what it is. Only the adult human being can be one thing and pretend to be another. When grown-ups punish a child for telling the truth, for revealing what they thinks and feels, the child learns to dissemble and differentiate, and their innocence is destroyed. Soon they will join the ranks of the numberless people who say helplessly, "I do not know who I am," for, having hidden the truth about themselves for so long from others, they end up by hiding it from themselves. How much of the innocence of childhood do you still retain? Is there anyone today in whose presence you can simply and totally be yourself, as nakedly open and innocent as a child?

There is another more subtle way in which the innocence of childhood is lost: when the child is infected by the desire to become somebody. Contemplate the crowds of people who are striving might and main to become not what Nature intended them to be—musicians, cooks, mechanics, carpenters, gardeners, inventors—but somebody successful, famous, powerful; to become something that will bring, not quiet self-fulfillment, but self-importance, self-absorption, self-seeking. You are looking at people who have lost their innocence because they have chosen not to be themselves but to promote themselves, to show off, even if it be only in their own eyes.

Look at your daily life. Is there a single thought, word, or action untainted by the desire to become somebody? Look at the ways you compare yourself with others, exchanging your simplicity for the ambition of wanting to be as good or better than someone else. The child, like the innocent animal, surrenders to its nature to be and become quite simply what it is. Adults who have preserved their innocence also surrender like the child to the impulse of Nature or Destiny without a thought to become somebody or to impress others; but, unlike the child, they rely, not on instinct, but on ceaseless awareness of everything in them and around them. That awareness shields them from ambitious egotism and brings about the growth that was intended for them by Nature, not designed by the vanity and arrogance of ego.

> "The moment you make the child a carbon copy you stamp out the spark of originality with which it came into the world.... Think sadly of the divine spark of uniqueness that lies within you, buried under layers of fear."

Another way grown-ups corrupt a child is they teach the child to imitate someone. The moment you make the child a carbon copy you stamp out the spark of originality with which they came into the world. You have prostituted their being.

Think sadly of the divine spark of uniqueness that lies within you, buried under layers of fear that you will be ridiculed or rejected if you dare to be yourself and refuse to conform mechanically to society's norms. See how you conform not only in your actions and thoughts but even in your reactions, your emotions, your attitudes, your values.

You dare not break out of this and reclaim your original innocence, and the price you pay is severe. It means you belong to the world of the crooked and the controlled, exiled from the kingdom of heaven that belongs to the innocence of childhood. Your life is spent not in living fully but in courting applause and admiration; not in blissfully being yourself but in neurotically comparing and competing and striving for worldly success, at times at the expense of defeating, humiliating, destroying your neighbors. This is the mechanical life that was stamped into you. Oh, this is hard language, but reflect on these words. Observe these negative impulses. When you're aware of them, you're free from them. They may raise their ugly heads, but you're not affected by it, you're not controlled by it. You've regained your natural urge to be free, your natural urge to love. That's the difference.

Self-Observation

When the Zen master attained enlightenment, he wrote the following lines to celebrate it:

> Oh wondrous marvel:
> I chop wood!
> I draw water from the well!

After enlightenment, nothing really changes. The tree is still a tree; people are just what they were before and so are you. You may continue to be as moody or even-tempered, as wise or foolish. The one difference is that you see things with a different eye. You are more detached from it all now. And your heart is full of wonder. That is the essence of contemplation: the sense of wonder. Contemplation is different from ecstasy in that ecstasy leads to withdrawal. The enlightened contemplative continues to chop wood and draw water from the well. Contemplation is different from the perception of beauty in that the perception of beauty (a painting or a sunset) produces aesthetic delight, whereas contemplation produces wonder—no matter what it observes, a sunset or a stone. This is the prerogative of children. They are so often in a state of wonder. So they easily slip into the Kingdom.

From *The Song of the Bird*

THIS WEEK, FOCUS ON THE FOLLOWING:

* When scientists investigate qualities that are fundamental to human nature, they often observe small children. So, whenever you are around small children, observe them. If you aren't around children this week, then rely on your memory of a child at play. Journal what you see or recall about the basic qualities children naturally demonstrate.
* Then answer these questions: What of the innocence of childhood do you still retain? What of the innocence of childhood have you lost? Is there anyone today in whose presence you can be simply and totally yourself, as nakedly open and innocent as a child?

NOTES TO MYSELF: _____

_____

_____

_____

_____

_____

_____

_____

_____

_____

_____

_____

_____

_____

WEEK 37

Passion is energy. Feel the power that comes from
focusing on what excites you.

—Oprah Winfrey

How many activities can you count in your life that you engage in simply because they delight you and grip your soul? You have probably been brainwashed into believing that your work only achieves maximum value if it becomes popular and sells, which means you are back again into the arms and control of people. The value of work, according to society, is not in its being loved, in its being done and enjoyed for itself, but in its achieving measurable success.

The royal road to mysticism, to enlightenment, to Reality does not pass through the world of people. It passes through the world of actions that are engaged in for themselves without an eye to success or to gain or their profit potential. They are actions that are engaged in out of love. Increasing love by extending it is the ultimate success in life. Love is gratuitousness. Like the tree, the rose, the lamp, the stars, it gives of itself without asking for anything in return. Think of the kind of feeling that came upon you when you saw an eagle fly over a lake or observed a flower peeping out of a crack in the wall or heard a baby laugh, each an unexpected gift that in your

> **The value of work, according to society, is not in its being loved, in its being done and enjoyed for itself, but in its achieving measurable success.**

heart you know will never be able to express the glory of what you saw or convey exactly what you felt.

You must cultivate activities that you love. You must discover work that you do, not for its utility, but for itself. Think of something that you love to do for itself, whether it succeeds or not, whether you are praised for it or not, whether you are loved and rewarded for it or not, whether people know about it and are grateful to you for it or not. Then make time to do them. Find the activities that grip your soul and cultivate them, for it is your passport to freedom and to love. Return to Nature: take some time out to gaze in wonder at the flight of a bird, a flower in bloom, the dry leaf crumbling to dust, the flow of a river, the rising of the moon, the silhouette of a mountain against the sky. Make time to enjoy the company of your friends and loved ones. Read a book or watch a movie that you thoroughly enjoy.

As you do these things, the hard, protective shell around your heart will soften and melt and your heart will come alive in sensitivity and responsiveness. The darkness in your eyes will be dispelled and your vision will become clear and penetrating, and you will know at last what love is.

Self-Observation

An ancient legend has it that when God was creating the world, He was approached by four angels. The first one asked, "How are you doing it?" The second, "Why are you doing it?" The third, "Can I be of help?" The fourth, "What is it worth?"

The first was a scientist; the second, a philosopher; the third, an altruist; and the fourth, a real estate agent.

A fifth angel watched in wonder and applauded in sheer delight. This one was the mystic.

From *The Prayer of the Frog*

THIS WEEK, FOCUS ON THE FOLLOWING:

* List activities you can begin right away, ones that engage your whole being, activities that you so love to do that while you're engaged in them time, success, recognition, and approval mean nothing to you.

* Then, as the week progresses, checkmark those you made time for. Journal about the inner qualities you experienced when you engaged in one or more of these activities. What did you feel? What change occurred in your attitude? What happened to your sense of time?

Notes to Myself: _____

_____

_____

_____

_____

_____

_____

_____

_____

_____

_____

_____

_____

WEEK 38

I want to think again of dangerous and noble things. I want to be light
and frolicsome. I want to be improbable beautiful and afraid of nothing,
as though I had wings.

—Mary Oliver

Life abhors security, for life means taking risks, exposing yourself to danger, even death. Jesus said that those who wish to be safe will lose their lives and those who are prepared to lose their lives will keep them.

When I think of the times when I drew back from taking risks, when I was comfortable and safe, those were times when I stagnated.

When I think of other times when I dared to take a chance, to make mistakes, to be a failure and a fool, to risk being criticized by others, when I dared to risk being hurt and causing pain to others, that is when I was alive!

Life is for the gambler. The coward dies. Life is at variance with my perception of what is good and bad: "These things are good and to be sought, and these others are bad and to be shunned." To eat of the Tree of Knowing Good and Bad is to fall from paradise.

We must learn to accept whatever life may bring, pleasure and pain, sorrow and joy. For if I close myself to pain, my capacity for pleasure dies, and I harden myself and repress what I regard as unpleasant and undesirable. And, in that hardness, that repression, is rigidity and death.

Taste, in all its fullness, the experience of the present moment, calling no experience good or bad. Those experiences that you dread, you think of them, and, inasmuch as you are able, let them come and stop resisting them.

Life goes hand in hand with change. What does not change is dead. Think of people who are fossils. Think of times when you were fossilized: no change, no newness, just repeating the same old worn-out concepts and

> **When I think of the times when I drew back from taking risks, when I was comfortable and safe, those were times when I stagnated.**

patterns of behavior, keeping the same mentality, neuroses, habits, prejudices.

The spiritually dead are rigid and fear change. Watch Nature. She is ever-changing, so flexible, so flowing, so vulnerable, a cycle of life and death that itself is so alive! Make Nature your teacher. Stand quietly before her, watching.

You will see in Nature what it is to be alive. Stand quietly before Nature and watch her for part of an hour or longer.

Self-Observation

A girl in the fishing village became an unwed mother and after several beatings finally revealed who the father of the child was: the Zen master living on the outskirts of the village.

The villagers trooped into the master's house, rudely disturbed his meditation, denounced him as a hypocrite, and told him to keep the baby. All the master said was, "Very well. Very well."

He picked the baby up and made arrangements for a woman from the village to feed and clothe and look after it at his expense.

The master's name was ruined and his disciples all abandoned him.

When this had gone on for a year, the girl who had borne the child could stand it no longer and finally confessed that she had lied. The father of the child was the boy next door.

The villagers were most contrite. They prostrated themselves at the feet of the master to beg his pardon and to ask for the child back. The master returned the child. And all he said was, "Very well. Very well."

From *The Song of the Bird*

THIS WEEK, FOCUS ON THE FOLLOWING:

* Recall a time when you drew back from taking a risk, when you played it safe. What happened? Then recall another time when you dared to take a chance, to make mistakes, to risk being a failure and a fool, to risk being criticized, when you dared to risk being hurt and challenging others. What happened then? Journal about both.

* What change in your life are you currently resisting or do you fear to make? Journal about it. Then sometime this week take that fear or resistance on a walk out in Nature and watch the way the fierce and gentle elements of Nature flow together, one with the other, creating ever-changing moments. Let it inspire you with courage to meet the change you want to make.

NOTES TO MYSELF: _____

_____

_____

_____

_____

_____

_____

_____

_____

_____

_____

_____

_____

_____

_____

_____

_____

_____

_____

_____

_____

_____

_____

_____

_____

_____

_____

_____

WEEK 39

To renounce things is not to give them up.
It is to acknowledge that all things go away.

—Shunryu Suzuki

Anytime you're practicing renunciation, you're deluded. How about that! You're deluded. What are you renouncing? Anytime you renounce something, you are tied forever to the thing you renounce. There's a guru in India who says, "Every time a prostitute comes to me, she's talking about nothing but God. She says, 'I'm sick of this life that I'm living. I want God.' But every time a priest comes to me he's talking about nothing but sex." When you renounce something, you're stuck to it forever. When you fight something, you're tied to it forever. As long as you're fighting it, you are giving it power. You give it as much power as you are using to fight it. You must "receive" your demons, because when you fight them, you empower them. When you renounce something, you're tied to it. The only way to get out of this is to see through it.

> One can use the material world and one can enjoy the material world but one does not make one's happiness depend on the material world.

Don't renounce the material world, see through it. Understand its true value and you won't need to renounce it; it will just drop from your hands. But of course, if you don't see that, if you're hypnotized into thinking that you won't be happy without this, that, or the other thing, you're stuck. What you need is not what so-called spirituality attempts to do—namely, to get you to make sacrifices, to renounce things. That's useless. You're still asleep. What you need is to understand, understand, understand. If you understood, you'd simply drop the desire for it. This is another way of saying: if you woke up, you'd simply drop the desire for it.

One can use the material world and one can enjoy the material world, but one does not make one's happiness depend on the material world. The irony is, when you are detached from the material world as you pursue success, you actually enjoy the process more than when you believe your worth, peace, and happiness depend on the outcome. If you succeed, great. If you fail, your happiness and self-worth are not at stake.

Self-Observation

A miser hid his gold at the foot of a tree in his garden. Every week he would dig it up and look at it for hours. One day a thief dug up the gold and made off with it. When the miser next came to gaze upon his treasure all he found was an empty hole.

The man began to howl with grief, so his neighbors came running to find out what the trouble was. When they found out, one of them asked, "Did you use any of the gold?"

"No," said the miser. "I only looked at it every week."

"Well, then," said the neighbor, "for all the good the gold did you, you might just as well come every week and gaze upon the hole."

From *The Prayer of the Frog*

THIS WEEK, FOCUS ON THE FOLLOWING:

* Journal about something of the material world you have a desire for and that you have renounced or think you should renounce. Can you see how fighting it gives it power?
* Consider what it means to you to use the material world and enjoy the material world but not to make your happiness depend on the material world. Journal about this too.

NOTES TO MYSELF: _____

_____

_____

_____

_____

_____

_____

_____

_____

_____

_____

_____

_____

_____

WEEK 40

People wait all week for Friday, all year for summer,
all life for happiness.

—Anonymous

Young or old, most of us are discontented merely because we want some-thing more: a better job, a finer car, a bigger salary. Our discontent is based upon our desire for "the more." It is only because we want something more that most of us are discontented.

Mostly the discontent that you feel comes from not having enough of something—you are dissatisfied because you think you do not have enough money or power or success or fame or virtue or love or holiness. This is not the discontent that leads to the joy of the kingdom. Its source is greed and ambition and its fruit is restlessness and frustration.

But I am not talking about that kind of discontent here. Yes, it is the desire for "the more" that prevents clear thinking, but if we are discontented not because we want something but without knowing what we want, we find that we are dissatisfied with our life, with our jobs, with making money, with seeking position and power, with tradition, with what

> **The day you are discontented not because you want more of something but because you are sick at heart of everything that you have been pursuing so far and you are sick of the pursuit itself, then your heart will attain a great clarity.**

237

we have and with what we might have. I am talking about feeling dissatisfied, not with anything in particular but with everything. Now, that is the kind of discontent that brings clarity.

When we don't accept or follow what we were told we should be, what we should want, and how the world should be, but instead question, investigate, and penetrate how we have been programmed from birth to be dissatisfied, ever striving, and rarely finding, there will be an insight out of which will come creativity, joy.

The day you are discontented not because you want more of something but because you are sick at heart of everything that you have been pursuing so far and you are sick of the pursuit itself, then your heart will attain a great clarity, an insight that will cause you to experience that mysterious moment when you delight in everything and in nothing.

Self-Observation

Buddha was once asked, "What makes a person holy?" He replied, "Every hour is divided into a certain number of seconds and every second into a certain number of fractions. Anyone who is able to be totally present in each fraction of a second is holy."

From *The Song of the Bird*

THIS WEEK, FOCUS ON THE FOLLOWING:

* Identify in yourself the kind of discontent that comes not from wanting something but from not knowing what you want; finding that you are dissatisfied with your life, with your jobs, with making money, with seeking position and power, with tradition, with what you have and with what you might have. Journal about it.

＊ Imagine for a moment that you stopped accepting or following what you were told about who you should be, what you should want, and how the world should be, but instead looked closely at how you have been programmed from birth to be dissatisfied with almost everything. What insights does that give you? Journal about it.

NOTES TO MYSELF: _____

_____

_____

_____

_____

_____

_____

_____

_____

_____

_____

_____

_____

WEEK 41

Do not suppress desire, because then you would become lifeless. You'd be without energy and that would be terrible. Because if you just suppress your desire, and you attempt to renounce the object of your desire, you are likely to be tied to it. Whereas if you look at it and see it for what it is really worth, if you understand how you are preparing the ground for misery and disappointment and depression, your desire will then be transformed into what I call a preference. When you go through life with preferences but don't let your happiness depend on any one of them, then you're awake. You're moving toward wakefulness. Wakefulness, happiness—call it what you wish—is the state of nondelusion, where you see things not as you are but as they are. To drop illusions is to see things, to see reality. Every time you are unhappy, you have added something to reality. It is that addition that makes you unhappy. Reality provides the stimulus; you provide the reaction. And if you examine what you have added, there is always an illusion there, there's a demand, an expectation, a craving. Always! Examples of illusions abound. But as you begin to move ahead on this path, you'll discover them for yourself. For instance, the illusion, the error of thinking that, by changing the exterior world, *you* will change. You do not change if you merely change your exterior world. If you get yourself a new job or a new spouse or a new home or a new guru or a new spirituality, that does not change you. It's like imagining that you change your capacity to think by changing your hat. But most people spend all their energies trying to rearrange their exterior world to suit their tastes. Sometimes they succeed—for about five minutes, because life is always flowing, life is always changing.

So if you want to live, you must flow with life. As the great Confucius said, "The one who would be constant in happiness must frequently change." Flow. But we keep looking back, don't we? We cling to things in the past and cling to things in the present. When you set your hand to the plow, you cannot look back. Do you want to enjoy a melody? Do you want to enjoy a symphony? Don't hold on to a few bars of the music. Let them pass, let them flow. The whole enjoyment of a symphony lies in your readiness to allow the notes to pass. The day you attain a posture like that, you will experience a miracle. You will change—effortlessly and correctly. Change will happen; you will not have to bring it about. If what you attempt is not to change yourself but to observe yourself—to study every one of your reactions to people and things without judgment, condemnation, or desire to reform yourself—your observations will be nonselective, comprehensive, never fixed on rigid conclusions, and always open and fresh from moment to moment. Then you will notice a marvelous thing happening within you: you will be flooded with the light of awareness. Negative feelings, every negative feeling, is useful for awareness, for understanding. They give you the opportunity to feel it, to watch it from the outside. In the beginning, the negativity, the upsets, will still be there, but you will have cut your connection with it. Gradually you will understand the upsets. As you understand it, it will occur less frequently, and will disappear altogether. Maybe, but by that time it won't matter too much. Before enlightenment I

> If what you attempt is not to change yourself but to observe yourself... then you will notice a marvelous thing happening within you: you will be flooded with the light of awareness.

used to be depressed. After enlightenment I continue to be depressed. But gradually, or rapidly, or suddenly, you get the state of wakefulness. This is the state where your happiness does not depend on the fulfillment of desire.

Self-Observation

The clock master was about to fix the pendulum of a clock when, to his surprise, he heard the pendulum speak.

"Please, sir, leave me alone," the pendulum pleaded. "It will be an act of kindness on your part. Think of the number of times I will have to tick day and night. So many times each minute, sixty minutes an hour, twenty-four hours a day, three hundred and sixty-five days a year. For year upon year . . . millions of ticks. I could never do it."

But the clock master answered wisely, "Don't think of the future. Just do one tick at a time and you will enjoy every tick for the rest of your life."

From *The Heart of the Enlightened*

THIS WEEK, FOCUS ON THE FOLLOWING:

* Each day, write about a desire you hold, then turn it into a preference by becoming clear that your happiness does not depend on attaining it. Journal about this process.
* At least once this week, sit down quietly and observe how your mind functions. There is a steady flow of thoughts and feelings and reactions there. Watch the whole of it for a good stretch of time the way you watch a river or a movie. Allow the unimpeded flow of things as they are that opens to the direct experience of Reality. Journal about this too.

Notes to Myself: _____

_____

_____

_____

_____

_____

_____

_____

_____

_____

_____

_____

_____

WEEK 42

The boys . . . went immediately to the candy case and stared in—
not with craving or with hope or even with desire,
but just with a kind of wonder that such things could be.
—John Steinbeck

An astronomer friend was recently telling me some of the fundamental things about astronomy. I did not know, until he told me, that when you see the sun, you're seeing it where it was eight and a half minutes ago, not where it is now. Because it takes a ray of the sun eight and a half minutes to get to us. So you're not seeing it where it is; it's now somewhere else. Stars, too, have been sending light to us for hundreds of thousands of years. So when we're looking at them, they may not be where we're seeing them; they may be somewhere else.

My friend said that, if we imagine a galaxy, a whole universe, this earth of ours would be lost toward the tail end of the Milky Way; not even in the center. Every one of the stars is a sun and some suns are so big that they could contain the sun and the earth and the distance between them. At a conservative estimate, there are one hundred million galaxies! The universe, as we know it, is expanding at the rate of two million miles a second.

> Awareness breaks loose into the kingdom of innocence where mystics and children dwell. . . . Reach out and take possession of the delight of a child moving out in wonder to discover the world.

I was fascinated listening to all of this, and when I came out of the restaurant, I looked up there and I had a different feel, a different perspective on life. That's awareness. So you can pick all this up as cold fact (and that's information), or suddenly you get another perspective on life—what are we, what's this universe, what's human life? When you get that feel, that's what I mean when I speak of awareness. Awareness breaks loose into the kingdom of innocence where mystics and children dwell. The reason the child is able to preserve its innocence and live like the rest of creation in the bliss of the kingdom is that they have not been sucked into what we call "the world," that region of darkness inhabited by grown-ups striving might and main for those empty things called success and fame. Reach out and take possession of the delight of a child moving out in wonder to discover the world.

Self-Observation

The Lord Krishna said to Arjuna, "You speak of me as of an incarnation of God. But today I wish to reveal something special to you. Follow me."

Arjuna followed the Lord a short distance. Then Krishna pointed to a tree and said, "What do you see there?"

Arjuna replied, "A huge vine with clusters of grapes hanging on it."

The Lord said, "Those are not grapes. Go closer and look at them carefully."

When Arjuna did that he could hardly believe his eyes for there before him were Krishnas hanging in bunches from Krishna.

The disciples asked the Master to speak to them of death: "What will it be like?"

"It will be as if a veil is ripped apart and you will say in wonder, 'So it was You all along.'"

From *The Prayer of the Frog*

THIS WEEK, FOCUS ON THE FOLLOWING:

＊ Every day this week, throughout the day, stop and stand still a few moments. Smell a rose. Watch how the sun encourages the grass to grow. Look at the sky. Gaze at the stars in the night sky and let the infinite eternity above you astonish you. Whenever you are in the presence of a child, silently observe the wonder in his or her eyes as they behold something you might regard as mundane or uninteresting. Later, journal about your experiences.

＊ At least once this week, take a walk into Nature and invite God to come along with you. Quiet your mind and allow your heart to open to all the wonders you often walk past. After, journal about your experiences.

NOTES TO MYSELF: _____

_____

_____

_____

_____

_____

_____

_____

_____

_____

_____

_____

_____

_____

WEEK 43

*If a man does not keep pace with his companions, perhaps it is because
he hears a different drummer. Let him step to the music which he hears,
however measured or far away.*

—Henry David Thoreau

One definition of an awakened person is someone who no longer marches to the drums of society, a person who dances to the tune of the music that springs up from within his or her own heart. Yet is there ever a minute when, consciously or unconsciously, you are not aware of or attuned to the reactions of others, marching to the beat of their drum?

> ... is there ever a minute when, consciously or unconsciously, you are not aware of or attuned to the reactions of others, marching to the beat of their drum?

When you are ignored or disapproved of, you experience a loneliness so unbearable that you crawl back to people and beg for the comforting drug called support and encouragement, reassurance. To live with people in this state involves a never-ending tension. "Hell is other people," said Sartre. How true. When you are in this state of dependency, you always have to be on your best behavior; you can never let your hair down; you've got to live up to expectations.

To be with people is to live in tension. But to be without them brings the agony of loneliness because you miss them. You have lost your capacity to see them exactly as they are and to respond to them accurately, because your perception of them is clouded by your need. It's an addiction. You're always looking at people, consciously or unconsciously, through these eyes. Will I get what I want from them, will I not get what I want from them?

And if they no longer support what you want, you're disillusioned with them. Round and round it goes. Can you imagine how liberating it would be to never be disillusioned again, never be disappointed again, never feel let down again? Never feel rejected?

Want to get off that treadmill? Want to wake up? Want freedom? Here it is: Drop your false ideas. See through people. If you see through yourself, you will see through everyone. Then you will be free. Then you will be able to love everyone.

✦

Self-Observation

When the Greek philosopher Diogenes was captured and taken to be sold in the slave market it is said that he mounted the auctioneer's platform and cried aloud, "A master has come here to be sold. Is there some slave among you who is desirous of purchasing him?"

From The Prayer of the Frog

THIS WEEK, FOCUS ON THE FOLLOWING:

* Take time this week to journal again on how liberating it would be for you to never be disillusioned again, never be disappointed again, never to feel rejected, never to be controlled by other people's judgments about you, who you should be, and what you should want.

* Allow yourself this week to see through yourself and the games you play for approval and how this mutes the sound of your own drum. Journal about it.

Notes to Myself: _____

_____

_____

_____

_____

_____

_____

_____

_____

_____

_____

_____

_____

_____

WEEK 44

A little too abstract, a little too wise,
It is time to kiss the earth again. . . .
I will touch things and things and no more thoughts.
—Robinson Jeffers

Here is a parable of life for you to ponder. A group of tourists sits in a bus that is passing through beautiful country, past lakes and mountains and green fields and rivers. But the window shades in the bus are pulled down. The passengers don't have the slightest idea about what lies outside the windows of the bus. The time of their journey is spent squabbling over who will have the seat of honor in the bus, who will be applauded, and who will be well considered. And so they remain until the journey's end.

Here is something you must understand: There are two sources for change within you. One is the cunningness of your ego; the other is the wisdom of Nature.

Your ego pushes you into making efforts to become something other than what you are meant to be so that it can glorify itself. The ego is a great technician but it cannot be creative. It goes in for methods and techniques and produces so-called holy people who are rigid, consistent, mechanical, lifeless, as intolerant of others as they are of themselves—violent people the very opposite of holiness and love. The type of "spiritual" people who, conscious of their spirituality, then proceed to crucify the Messiah.

That is not the way of Nature. Nature is not a technician. Nature is creative. You will be a creator, not the wily technician, when there is abandonment in you. In Nature there is no greed, no ambition, no anxiety, no sense of striving, gaining, arriving, attaining. All there is, is a keen, alert, penetrating, vigilant awareness that causes the dissolution of all one's foolishness and selfishness, all one's attachments and fears. Observe the wisdom that operates in doves and in flowers and trees and the whole of Nature. It is the same wisdom that circulates our blood, digests our food, pumps our heart, expands our lungs, immunizes our bodies, and heals our wounds while our conscious minds are engaged in other matters. This kind of Nature wisdom we are only now beginning to discover in so-called primitive peoples who, like the doves, are so simple and wise.

> "Your ego pushes you into making efforts to become something other than what you are meant to be so that it can glorify itself. The ego is a great technician but it cannot be creative."

When your body is too long withdrawn from the elements, it withers, it becomes flabby and fragile because it has been isolated from its life force. When you are too long separated from Nature, your spirit withers and dies because it has been wrenched from its roots.

❖

Self-Observation

Once upon a time there was a forest where the birds sang by day and the insects by night. Trees flourished, flowers bloomed, and all manner of creatures roamed about in freedom.

And all who entered there were led to Solitude, which is the home of God who dwells in Nature's silence and Nature's beauty.

But then the Age of Unconsciousness arrived when it became possible for people to construct buildings a thousand feet high and to destroy rivers and forests and mountains in a month. So houses of worship were built from the wood of the forest trees and from the stone under the forest soil. Pinnacle, spire, and minaret pointed toward the sky; the air was filled with the sound of bells, with prayer and chant and exhortation.

And God was suddenly without a home.

From *The Prayer of the Frog*

THIS WEEK, FOCUS ON THE FOLLOWING:

* Step out into Nature again this week, even if it is only a walk down a tree-lined neighborhood. Observe how flexible Nature is, so flowing, so fragile, so exposed to death—and so alive! As you walk along doing this, ask yourself: "How in touch am I with Nature, with trees and earth and grass and sky and wind and rain and sun and flowers and birds and animals?" Ask yourself, "How much am I exposed to Nature? How much do I commune with her, observe her, contemplate her in wonder, identify with her?"

* If you need a creative insight to solve a problem, whatever the problem, take a walk among the trees and birds and sky, quieting your mind as you walk along, being fully present, open to the world around you. Afterward, when you are at your desk, be aware of how rejuvenated you are and how creative your thinking has become in approaching the task or problem in front of you.

NOTES TO MYSELF: _____

WEEK 45

That it will never come again is what makes life so sweet.

—Emily Dickinson

Has it ever struck you that those who most fear to die are the ones who most fear to live? That in running away from death we are running away from life?

Think of a man living in an attic, a little hole of a place with no light and little ventilation. He fears to come down the stairs because he has heard of people falling down stairs and breaking their necks. He would never cross a street because he has heard of thousands who have been run over on the streets. This man clings to his hole of an attic in the attempt to ward off death and in doing so he has simultaneously warded off life. For life is on the move and he is stuck, life flows and he has become stagnant, life is flexible and free and he is rigid and frozen. Life carries all things away and he craves stability and permanence. He fears life and he fears death because he clings. When you cling to nothing, when you have no fear of losing anything, then you are free to flow like the mountain stream that is always fresh and sparkling and alive.

I've often said to people that the way to really live is to die. If you're protecting your life, you're dead. If you're sitting up there in the attic and I say to you, "Come on down!" and you say, "No," and I can't get you to peep out of your little narrow beliefs and convictions and look at another world, you're dead, you're completely dead; life has passed you by. You're sitting in your little prison, where you're frightened, where you're going to lose your God, your religion, your friends, all kinds of things.

Life is for the gambler—it really is. That's what Jesus was saying. Are you ready to risk your life? Do you know when you're ready to risk it?

> You're not living until it doesn't matter a tinker's damn to you whether you live or die.... Love the thought of death, love it. Go back to it again and again.

It is when you discover that this anxious existence people call life is not really life; when you know that you have to take risks to live life fully. We live in a flash of light—only a flash—and we waste it with our anxiety, our worries, our concerns, and our burdens. People mistakenly think that living is only about keeping the body alive, and every time I challenge them to look at death, they say, "How disgusting!" They don't want to relate to death. They're too frightened to think of it. You're not living until it doesn't matter a tinker's damn to you whether you live or die. At that point you truly live. When you're ready to lose your life, you begin to live it. It's such a relief when you can look on life from that perspective. It wakes you up. So love the thought of death, love it. Go back to it again and again.

Self-Observation

Here is a parable that the Lord Buddha told his disciples: A man came across a tiger in a field. The tiger gave chase and the man fled. He came upon a precipice, stumbled, and began to fall. Then he reached out and caught hold of a little strawberry bush that was growing along the side of the precipice.

There he hung for some minutes, suspended between the hungry tiger above and the deep chasm below where he was soon going to meet his death.

Suddenly he spied a luscious strawberry growing on the bush. Grasping the bush with one hand, he plucked the strawberry with the other and put it into his mouth. Never in his life had a strawberry tasted so sweet!

From *The Prayer of the Frog*

THIS WEEK, FOCUS ON THE FOLLOWING:

* Imagine you're lying flat on a slab and you're dead. You see the body decomposing, then bones, then dust. Now look at your problems from that viewpoint. Do this meditation a few times this week and journal about it. I guarantee you, you'll come alive.

* Find time to visit a cemetery. It's not a macabre experience; it's an enormously purifying and beautiful experience. You look at the dates and names on the tombstones of people who lived so many decades ago, maybe centuries ago. Consider that they must have had all the problems that you have, must have had lots of sleepless nights. Figure out the ages of the people buried there and reflect on how long life sometimes seems and yet, in truth, how we actually live for such a short time.

NOTES TO MYSELF: _____

_____

_____

_____

_____

_____

_____

_____

_____

_____

_____

_____

_____

_____

PART 4

THE ME, THE I, AND GOD

We are, all of us, endowed with a mystical mind and mystical heart.
These are faculties that make it possible for us to know God directly,
to grasp and intuit Him in His very being . . . apart from all thoughts
and concepts and images.

—**Anthony De Mello**

WEEK 46

The great masters tell us that the most important question in the world is: "Who am I?" Or rather: "What is 'I'?" What is this thing I call "I"? What is this thing I call "self"? Do you mean we understood everything else in the world and we didn't understand this? Again and again in my therapy groups I come across people who aren't there at all. Their daddy is there, their mommy is there, but they're not there. They never were there. I would ask, "Now, this sentence, does it come from Daddy, Mommy, Grandma, Grandpa, whom?" We think we are free, but there probably isn't a gesture, a thought, an emotion, an attitude, a belief in you that isn't coming from someone else, and you don't even know it.

Be aware a moment of your presence in this room, as if you were out-side yourself looking at yourself. Notice you've got "I" observing "me." That the "I" can observe "me" is a phenomenon that has never ceased to amaze philosophers, mystics, and scientists alike. It raises the question, What's an "I"? What is a "me"? What I'm going to give you now is not metaphysics; it is not philosophy. It is plain observation and common sense. Listen to this: Am I my thoughts, the thoughts that I am thinking? No. Thoughts come and go; I am not my thoughts.

Am I my body? They tell us that millions of cells in our bodies are changed or are renewed every minute, and that by the end of seven years, we don't have a single living cell in our bodies that was there seven years before. Cells come and go. Cells arise and die—but "I" seems to persist. So am I my body? Evidently not! "I" is something other and more than the body. You might say the body is part of "I," but it is a changing part. It keeps moving, it keeps changing. It is an ever-changing reality.

How about my name? Is "I" my name? Evidently not, because I can change my name without changing the "I." How about my career? Not there either, because I can change my career without changing the "I."

How about when I say, "I am successful." Is your success part of the "I"? No, successes come and go; they could be here today and gone tomorrow. That's not "I." The same thing is true when you say, "I am a failure."

> Suffering exists in "me," so when you identify "I" with "me," suffering begins. Attachment begins. Illusion begins. You have identified with a fabrication.

How about my beliefs? I say I am a certain religion—is that an essential part of "I"? When I move from one religion to another, has the "I" changed? Do I have a new "I," or is it the same "I" that has changed? In other words, is my name an essential part of me, of the "I"? Is my religion an essential part of the "I"?

The fact is that whatever labels you think of (except perhaps "human being") should be applied to "me," "I" is none of these labels. When you step out of yourself and observe "me," you no longer identify with "me." Suffering exists in "me," so when you identify "I" with "me," suffering begins. Attachment begins. Illusion begins. You have identified with a fabrication. When "I" does not identify with money, or name, or nationality, or titles, or persons, or friends, or any quality, nothing threatens you. What is real and true within you is never threatened. The "I" can be very active, but whatever happens, it is not threatened.

Self-Observation

Disciple: I have come to offer you my service.

Master: If you dropped the "I," service would automatically follow.

You could give all your goods to feed the poor and your body to be burned and not have love at all. Keep your goods and abandon the "I." Don't burn your body; burn the ego. Love will automatically follow.

From *The Song of the Bird*

THIS WEEK, FOCUS ON THE FOLLOWING:

* Look at yourself as if you were watching another person, then write down on a piece of paper in brief terms any way you would describe yourself. For example: doctor, lawyer, businessperson, spouse, parent, priest, Catholic, Jew. Anything. See these labels as a phenomenon called "me."

* Now, notice you've got "I" observing "me." Recall how your "me" has changed over time. Understand that what constantly changes is "me." Next, think of anything that caused or is causing you pain, worry, or anxiety. Pick up the desire under that suffering—that there's something you desire very keenly or else you wouldn't be suffering. What is that desire? It isn't simply a desire; there's an identification there. You have somehow said to yourself, "The well-being of 'I'—the existence of 'I'—is tied up with this desire." Then ask yourself, "Who am I without these transient things?" Journal about this.

NOTES TO MYSELF: _____

_____

_____

_____

_____

_____

_____

_____

_____

_____

_____

_____

_____

_____

_____

WEEK 46

WEEK 47

Awareness is like the sun. When it shines on things,
they are transformed.

—Thich Nhat Hanh

There's nothing so delightful as being aware. Would you rather live in darkness? Would you rather act and not be aware of your actions, talk and not be aware of your words? Would you rather listen to people and not be aware of what you're hearing, or see things and not be aware of what you're looking at? That's a self-evident truth. Socrates said that the unaware life is not worth living. But most people don't live aware lives. They live mechanical lives, mechanical thoughts—generally somebody else's—mechanical emotions, mechanical actions, mechanical reactions.

Do you want to see how mechanical you really are? "My, that's a lovely shirt you're wearing." You feel proud of yourself when you hear that. Over a shirt, for heaven's sake! People come over to my center in India and they say, "What a lovely place, these lovely trees, this lovely climate," for which I'm not responsible at all, and already I'm feeling good. That is until I catch myself feeling good, and I think, *Hey, can you imagine anything as silly as that?* I'm not responsible for those trees. I didn't order the weather; it just happened. But "me" got in there, so I'm feeling good. Someone compliments my great Indian culture for producing all the great mystics and now I'm feeling good about "my" culture and "my" nation. How absurd is that. I didn't produce those mystics. I'm not responsible for them. Someone else says the opposite. They tell me, "That country of yours and its poverty; it's disgusting." I feel ashamed. But I didn't create it. One person presses a button and I'm up; someone else presses another button and I'm down. People tell you something nice and you feel wonderful; you got a positive stroke. That's what psychology calls "I'm OK, you're OK." I'm going to write a book someday and title it *I'm an Ass, You're an Ass*. By "ass" I mean when "me" steps into the picture and everything gets fouled up. That's when you become selfish and insensitive, misperceiving people and events and overreacting in ways that makes you look like an ass. When you so identify with "me" then there's too much of "me" in it for you to see things with the intelligent detachment of the "I."

What kills sensitivity is the conditioned self. That's the "me." It lives to fulfill other people's expectations, and as long as it does, you better watch what you wear, how you comb your hair, whether your shoes are polished. In short, the "me" makes you live up to every asinine expectation that society has programmed into you. Seeing

> **You will be delighted to discover that for growth and transformation, it is enough simply to be watchful and awake.**

what an ass it has made of you can be horrifying. Openly admitting you're an ass is the most liberating, wonderful thing in the world. In the final liberation, I'm an ass, you're an ass. Now, whenever people tell you you're wrong, you can say, "What would you expect of an ass?" Cut out all the OK stuff and the not-OK stuff. How? Simply observe, just watch. Give time to the "I" observing "me."

Allow into awareness every one of your reactions to people and things and the world, without judgment or condemnation or the desire to reform yourself. Let your observation be nonselective, comprehensive, never fixed on rigid conclusions, always open and fresh from moment to moment. You will be delighted to discover that for growth and transformation, it is enough simply to be watchful and awake Then you will notice a marvelous thing happening within you: you will be flooded with the light of awareness; you will become transparent and transformed.

Self-Observation

No Zen student would presume to teach others until he had lived with his master for at least ten years. Tenno, having completed his ten years of apprenticeship, acquired the rank of teacher. One day he went to visit the master Nan-in. It was a rainy day, so Tenno wore wooden clogs and carried an umbrella. When he walked in, Nan-in greeted him with, "You left your wooden clogs and umbrella on the porch, didn't you? Tell me, did you place your umbrella on the right side of the clogs or on the left?" Tenno was embarrassed, for he did not know the answer. He realized he lacked awareness. So he became Nan-in's student and labored for another ten years to acquire constant awareness.

The person who is ceaselessly aware; the person who is totally present at each moment: behold the master!

From *The Song of the Bird*

THIS WEEK, FOCUS ON THE FOLLOWING:

* Journal about all the ways the "me" seeks to fulfill people's expectations of you, the "me's" concern with appearances, how you're emotionally high when someone else compliments "me" and emotionally low when someone else ignores "me," rejects "me," or is disinterested in "me." See how this places you at the mercy of things and people as you try desperately to win approval. Investigate it with the aim of understanding what is driving it.

* Spend each day this week consciously cutting out all the OK stuff and the not-OK stuff that goes on in your head, simply by allowing it into awareness, observing it without judging it or believing it or identifying with any of it, and watching as it eventually passes.

NOTES TO MYSELF: _____

_____

_____

_____

_____

_____

_____

_____

_____

_____

_____

_____

_____

WEEK 48

Shame, blame, disrespect, betrayal, and the withholding of affection
damage the roots from which love grows.

—Brené Brown

Someone once said, "The three most difficult things for a human being are not physical feats or intellectual achievements. They are first, returning love for hate; second, including the excluded; and third, admitting that you are wrong." But these are the easiest things in the world if you haven't identified with the programmed, conditioned self . . . with the "me," as I have been calling it. Look behind these three reactions and you will see there is an identification there. When there's too much of "me" in a situation, everything gets fouled up. You cannot see clearly. Negative emotion produced by attachment kills sensitivity and we launch into fear and blame.

Any time you have a negative feeling toward anyone, including yourself, you're living in an illusion. You're not seeing reality. We always hate what we fear. We want to destroy and get rid of and avoid what we fear. You hate a person insofar as you fear that person. In every situation, what you need is to be free; what you need is to love. That's your nature; that's everyone's nature; that's reality.

Dare to look at everything around you without fear and desire, and love will arise, and you will see that love is never threatened; love never attacks or defends. The "I" is never threatened; it's only "me" that is threatened. Detach and you become very sensitive to things and people around you. Even if someone hates or excludes you, your loving eyes will see the divine spark that lies within that person, buried under layers of fear. And if you made a mistake or behaved poorly, you will be able to say something like, "I'm wrong! If you knew me better, you'd see how often I'm wrong,"

285

But there will be no shame, not with love; your worth will not come into question. There will be none of "He's to blame," or "It wasn't me; I'm not to blame," or "She has to change." You'll see that the one who has to change at the moment is you.

How? It's very important before you swing into action to see things with detachment, for only detachment releases love. Many wrongly assume that not having negative feelings like anger and resentment, vengeance and hate, guilt and shame means that you do nothing about a situation that calls for action. Oh no, oh no! When negative feelings come in, you go blind. Detach and your mind will become clear and unclouded by fear or desire and suddenly you'll be unaffected emotionally by the situation. Negative emotions prevent that.

> "Many wrongly assume that not having negative feelings like anger and resentment, vengeance and hate, guilt and shame means that you do nothing about a situation that calls for action. Oh no, oh no!"

How, then, you might ask, do I relate with the kind of passion that motivates or activates me into doing something about objective evils, like seeing someone injuring a child? Whatever the situation, if we are in touch with love, when we spring into action it will not be a reaction; it will be action. It may be that the old negative conditioning will kick in initially. But now because of awareness there will be a difference. You won't identify with the reaction; you won't identify with the upset; you won't be controlled by "me." You'll step outside of yourself and look at "me' and let it be as it is while it passes through you and disappears. You're now willing to let this cloud come in, because you have seen the more you fight it, the more power you give it, so you are willing to observe it as it passes by. You have seen that "I" is not troubled by it. There is no quarrel with anyone, no jealousies, no conflicts, no hate, no shame.

Self-Observation

A former inmate of a Nazi concentration camp was visiting a friend who had shared the ordeal with him. "Have you forgiven the Nazis?" he asked his friend.

"Yes."

"Well, I haven't. I'm still consumed with hatred for them."

"In that case," said his friend gently, "they still have you in prison."

From *The Heart of the Enlightened*

THIS WEEK, FOCUS ON THE FOLLOWING:

* This week, keep the "three most difficult things for a human being" in front of you, (i.e., returning love for hate, including the excluded, and admitting you were wrong). Write them down and place them where you'll be reminded of them. Then, if you should find yourself hating someone or excluding someone or being stubborn about admitting a mistake, be aware that you have identified with the programmed, conditioned self, and remember that when there's too much of "me" in a situation it's bound to kill sensitivity and foul things up.

* Welcome the challenge of detaching from the "me." Don't identify with the emotions that "me" is causing by observing them as if you were watching another person. This will help you see the upset is in you, not in reality. At the same time, don't do a thing to make "me" go away; just be willing to allow its negativity to pass through you

287

and disappear. Then respond to the situation by either returning love for hate, including someone you just excluded, or admitting that you made a mistake. Journal about all this.

WEEK 48

NOTES TO MYSELF: _____

_____

_____

_____

_____

_____

_____

_____

_____

_____

_____

_____

_____

_____

WEEK 49

We need no wings to go in search of [God] but have only to . . .
look upon Him present within us.

—St. Teresa of Ávila

Mystics tell us that, in addition to the mind and heart with which we ordinarily communicate with God, we are, all of us, endowed with a mystical mind and mystical heart. These are faculties that make it possible for us to know God directly, to grasp and intuit Him in His very being, though in a dark manner, apart from all thoughts and concepts and images. You are surrounded by God, yet you don't see God because you "know" about God. The final barrier to the vision of God is your God concept. You miss God because you think you know. The great Chinese sage Lao Tzu said, "The one who knows does not say; the one who says does not know."

God cannot be described. For example, suppose that I'd never smelled a rose before, and I asked you what the fragrance of a rose smelled like. Could you describe it for me? Of course not. Well, if you cannot describe a simple thing like the fragrance of the rose, how could you describe the Almighty? Whatever words you would use would fall short. Any image that your mind makes will be more unlike God than like God. The experience of God is totally beyond description or imagination.

> **Any image that your mind makes will be more unlike God than like God. The experience of God is totally beyond description or imagination.**

291

There is far too much God talk and the world is sick of it. There's too little dropping of illusions, dropping of errors, dropping of attachments and cruelty, too little awareness. That's what the world is suffering from. The highest knowledge of God is to know God as unknowable.

All revelations, however divine, are never any more than a finger pointing to the moon. As it is said in the East, "When the sage points to the moon, all the idiot sees is the finger."

So, the first thing in connecting to God is to acknowledge that your ideas of God are all inadequate. St. Thomas Aquinas in the prologue of his *Summa Theologica* wrote this: "About God, we cannot say what He is but rather what He is not. And so we cannot speak about how He is but rather how He is not." And in his famous commentary on Boethius's *De Sancta Trinitate*, Thomas says there are three ways of knowing God: (1) in the creation, (2) in God's actions through history, and (3) in the highest form of the knowledge of God—to know God as the unknown.

Self-Observation

Hindu India developed a magnificent image to describe God's relationship with creation. God "dances" creation. He is the dancer; creation is his dance. The dance is different from the dancer, yet it has no existence apart from him. You cannot take it home in a box if it pleases you. The moment the dancer stops, the dance ceases to be. In our quest for God, we think too much, reflect too much, talk too much. Even when we look at this dance that we call creation, we are the whole time thinking, talking (to ourselves and others), reflecting, analyzing, philosophizing. Words. Noise. Be silent and contemplate the dance. Just look: a star, a flower, a fading leaf, a bird, a stone . . . any fragment of the dance will do. Look. Listen. Smell.

Touch. Taste. And, hopefully, it won't be long before you see him—the dancer himself!

From *The Song of the Bird*

THIS WEEK, FOCUS ON THE FOLLOWING:

* Recall moments in your life when your mystical heart opened to an experience that you will carry with you for life, something you are quite powerless to express in words, much less convey in fullness to another human being. It could be as simple as the feeling that came over you when you saw a bird fly over a lake, or a flower sprouting out of a crack in the concrete of a city sidewalk, or when you we were moved by the loveliness of a naked human body, or when you gazed at a corpse lying lifeless and rigid in a coffin.

* Sit with the feeling of the mystical heart. Drop your God concepts and open to the fact that you're surrounded by God. Open to reality. Reality is lovely; it is an absolute delight. Eternal life is now.

NOTES TO MYSELF: _____

_____

_____

_____

_____

_____

_____

_____

_____

_____

_____

_____

_____

WEEK 50

It is only when I am alone and calm that I am able to communicate
with God, for He cannot reach me when I am in turmoil.

—A.A. Daily Reflections

To be able to grasp God beyond thoughts and images is the privilege of
this faculty which I shall call the Heart, though it has nothing to do with
our physical heart or our affectivity.

In most of us, this Heart lies dormant and undeveloped. If it were to
be awakened, it would be constantly straining toward God and, given a
chance, would impel the whole of our being toward God. But for this, the
Heart needs to be developed, it needs to have the dross that surrounds it
removed so that it can be attracted toward the Eternal Magnet. The dross
is the vast number of thoughts and words and images that we constantly
interpose between ourselves and God when we are communicating with
Him. Words sometimes serve to impede rather than foster communication
and intimacy.

Silence—of words and thoughts—can sometimes be the most powerful form of communication and union when hearts are full of love. Our
communication with God, however, is not quite so simple a matter. I can
gaze lovingly into the eyes of an intimate friend and communicate with
him beyond words. But what do I gaze into when I gaze silently at God?
An imageless, formless reality. A blank! Now that is just what is demanded
of some people if they would go deep into communion with the Infinite,
with God: gaze for hours at a blank. Some mystics recommend that we
gaze at this blank lovingly. When first reaching for God, it requires a good
deal of faith to gaze with love and yearning at what seems like just nothing. But if your mind isn't silenced, you will never even get anywhere near

this blank, even supposing you muster up an intense willingness to spend hours on end gazing at it. As long as your mind machine keeps spinning out millions of thoughts and words, your mystical mind, your mystical heart remains underdeveloped. "Silence is the great revelation," said Lao Tzu. And so it is.

If you ever come to union with God, you must pass through silence. The experience of people who attempt silence is infinitely varied. Most people discover that silence is something to which they are not accustomed. They cannot still the constant mind wandering or quiet an emotional turmoil. Others feel themselves approaching the frontiers of silence and then panic and withdraw. Silence can be frightening; the blank nothingness can also be frightening. No reason to be discouraged. Even those wandering thoughts are a great revelation about yourself.

> "When first reaching for God, it requires a good deal of faith to gaze with love and yearning at what seems like just nothing. But if your mind isn't silenced, you will never even get anywhere near this blank."

And here's some more encouragement for you: the fact that you were aware of your mental wanderings or your inner turmoil or your inability to be still shows that you have at least a sufficient amount of silence to be aware of all of it. But it is not enough to know this. You must take time to experience this wandering mind, and the type of wandering it indulges in. Oh, how revealing that will be for you as well!

Self-Observation

A priest's daughter asked him where he got the ideas for his sermons.

"From God," he replied.

"Then why do I see you scratching things out?" asked the girl.

From *The Heart of the Enlightened*

THIS WEEK, FOCUS ON THE FOLLOWING:

* When you come to sit before God, take a comfortable posture and close your eyes and relax. Next, invoke your mystical heart by recalling a moment when it opened wide. Recall the feeling that came over you when you saw something as simple as a bird flying over a lake, or something as profound as the birth of a child or the peace on the face of someone who just died. Be present in silence with that feeling. Just become sensitively aware and silence will appear.

* If you now wish to communicate with God within this silence, imagine that you surrender, letting go completely to this intention. Follow your breath and see each exhalation as your way of saying yes to God. Say yes to the being God created you to become. Say yes to the whole of your past. Say yes to the future that lies in store for you. Let go each time you breathe out with the awareness that you are in God's hands and that all is well. Let all anxiety cease and let peace take over, for in God's hands, in His will, is your peace. Keep silent for a period of ten minutes, being aware of whatever revelation the silence brings.

This concludes the Self-Observation exercises; however, you can still make notes to yourself at the end of each of the chapters that follow.

Notes to Myself: _____

_____

_____

_____

_____

_____

_____

_____

_____

_____

_____

_____

_____

PART 5

FAITH

Love is generated through awareness and through no other way,
no other way. . . . Turn on the light of awareness and the
darkness will disappear.

—Anthony De Mello

WEEK 51

C. S. Lewis wrote a diary while his wife was dying. It's called *A Grief Observed*. He had married an American woman whom he loved dearly. He told his friends, "God gave me in my sixties what He denied me in my twenties." He hardly had married her when she died a painful death of cancer. Lewis said that his whole faith crumbled, like a house of cards. Here he was the great Christian apologist, but when disaster struck home, he asked himself, "Is God a loving Father or is God the great vivisectionist?" There's pretty good evidence for both! Lewis said that he never had any doubts before about God, but when his wife died, he was no longer certain. Why? Because, of course, it was so important to him that his beloved be living.

I remember that when my own mother got cancer, my sister said to me, "Tony, why did God allow this to happen to Mother?" I said to her, "My dear, last year a million people died of starvation in China because of the drought, and you never raised a question." Sometimes the best thing that can happen to us is to be awakened to reality, for calamity to strike, for then we come to faith stronger in it, as C. S. Lewis did.

There is nothing so cruel as nature. Can one be fully human without experiencing tragedy? The only tragedy there is in the world is ignorance; all evil comes from that. The only tragedy there is in the world is unwakefulness and unawareness. From them comes fear, and from fear comes every other evil. Richard Bach said, "The mark of your ignorance is the depth of your belief in injustice and tragedy. What the caterpillar calls the end of the world,

303

the master calls a butterfly." Death is resurrection. We're talking not about some resurrection that will happen but about one that is happening right now. If you would die to the past, if you would die to every minute, you would be the person who is fully alive, because a fully alive person is one who is full of death. We're always dying to things. We're always shedding everything in order to come home to ourselves, in order to be fully alive and to be resurrected at every moment.

We're always bothered by the tragic, by the problem of evil. Life is a mystery, which means your thinking mind cannot make sense out of it. For that you've got to wake up and then you'll suddenly realize that reality is not problematic; your programmed reaction to it is the problem.

It's worth mentioning again the words in the *Bhagavad Gita* that Lord Krishna gave to Arjuna: "Plunge into the heat of battle and keep your heart at the lotus feet of the Lord." A marvelous sentence. It's not your actions, it's

> in the *Bhagavad Gita* … Lord Krishna [says] to Arjuna, "Plunge into the heat of battle and keep your heart at the lotus feet of the Lord." A marvelous sentence. It's not your actions, it's your being that counts.

your being that counts. It is an openness to the truth, no matter what the consequences, no matter where it leads you and when you don't even know where it's going to lead you. That's faith. Not belief, but faith. Your beliefs give you a lot of security, but faith is insecurity. You don't know. You're ready to follow and you're open, you're wide open! You're ready to listen. And mind you, being open does not mean being gullible, it doesn't mean swallowing whatever some teacher is saying. You've got to challenge everything; you've got to sit with it and see if it resonates in your heart.

NOTES TO MYSELF: _____

_____

_____

_____

_____

_____

_____

_____

_____

_____

_____

_____

_____

_____

_____

_____

_____

_____

_____

_____

_____

_____

_____

_____

_____

WEEK 52

There is no explanation you can give that would explain away all the sufferings and injustice and torture and destruction and hunger in the world! You'll never explain it. There's a powerful story about a little boy walking along the bank of a river. He sees a crocodile who is trapped in a net. The crocodile says, "Would you have pity on me and release me? I may look ugly, but it isn't my fault, you know. I was made this way. But whatever my external appearance, I have a mother's heart. I came this morning in search of food for my young ones and got caught in this trap!" So the boy says, "Ah, if I were to help you out of that trap, you'd grab me and kill me." The crocodile asks, "Do you think I would do that to my benefactor and liberator?" So the boy is persuaded to take the net off and the crocodile grabs him. As he is being forced between the jaws of the crocodile, he says, "So this is what I get for my good actions." And the crocodile says, "Well, don't take it personally, son—this is the way the world is; this is the law of life." The boy sees a bird sitting on a branch and says, "Bird, is what the crocodile says right?" The bird says, "The crocodile is right. Look at me. I was coming home one day with food for my fledglings. Imagine my horror to see a snake devouring my young ones." "See," says the crocodile.

"I was good to you, so give me one last chance," the boy says. "Let me ask one other being if this is the way of world." So the crocodile says, "All right, one last chance." The boy sees a rabbit passing by, and he asks the rabbit if the crocodile is right. The rabbit sits on his haunches and says to the crocodile, "We've got to discuss this, but how can we discuss it when you've got that boy in your mouth? Release him so he can take part in the discussion too." The crocodile says, "You're a clever one, you are. The moment I release him, he'll run away." The rabbit says, "You surely have more sense than that. You know if he attempted to run away, one slash of your tail would kill him." "Fair enough," says the crocodile, and he releases the boy. The moment the boy is released, the rabbit says, "Run!" And the boy runs to the village and calls all the menfolk. They come with axes and staves and spears and they kill and butcher the crocodile and have a banquet. The boy's dog comes, too, and when the dog sees the rabbit, he gives chase, catches hold of the rabbit, and throttles him. The boy arrives on the scene too late, when his dog is in the frenzy of the kill and cannot be stopped, and the boy watches in horror as the rabbit dies. "The crocodile was right," he says to his mother. "This is the way the world is; this is the law of life."

> There is no explanation you can give that would explain away all the sufferings and injustice and torture and destruction and hunger in the world! You'll never explain it.

There is nothing so cruel as nature. You can try gamely with your formulas, religious and otherwise, but you'll never explain it. Everything that seems on the surface to be a curse may be a good in disguise. And everything that seems a blessing on the surface may really be a curse. So we are wise when we leave it to God to decide what is good and what is bad and thank Him that all things turn out a blessing with those who love Him. Then we will share something of that marvelous mystical vision of Julian of Norwich, who uttered the loveliest and most consoling words I have ever read: "All shall be well and all shall be well and all manner of things shall be well."

Notes to Myself: _____

_____

_____

_____

_____

_____

_____

_____

_____

_____

_____

_____

_____

_____

_____

PART 6

ONE LAST WORD—
ALL IS WELL

There is a lovely sentence from scripture about everything turning i
nto good for those who love God. What that means to me is that
when you finally awaken, you don't try to make good things happen;
they just happen.

—**Anthony De Mello**

THE COMING YEAR

> You do not walk alone. God's angels hover near and all about. His Love surrounds you, and of this be sure: that [Christ] will never leave you comfortless.
>
> —*A Course in Miracles*

There's a famous story about the lion who came upon a flock of sheep and to his amazement found a lion among the sheep. It was a lion who had been brought up by the sheep ever since he was a cub. He would bleat like a sheep and run around like a sheep. The lion went straight for him, and when the sheep-lion stood in front of the real one, he trembled in every limb. And the lion said to him, "What are you doing among these sheep?" And the sheep-lion said, "I am a sheep." And the lion said, "Oh no you're not. You're coming with me." So he took the sheep-lion to a pool and said, "Look!" And when the sheep-lion looked at his reflection in the water, he let out a mighty roar, and in that moment he was transformed. He was never the same again.

There is a lovely sentence from scripture about everything turning into good for those who love God. What that means to me is that when you finally awaken, you don't try to make good things happen; they just happen. If you're lucky and the gods are gracious or if you are gifted with divine grace (use any theological expression you want), you might suddenly understand who "I" is, and you'll never be the same again, never. Nothing will ever be able to touch you again and no one will ever be able to hurt you again.

You will fear no one and you will fear nothing. Isn't that extraordinary? You'll live like a king, like a queen. This is what it means to live like royalty. Not rubbish like getting your picture in the newspapers or having a lot of

313

money. That's a lot of rot. You fear no one because you're perfectly content to be nobody. You don't give a damn about success or failure. They mean nothing. Honor, disgrace, they mean nothing! If you make a fool of yourself, that means nothing either. Isn't that a wonderful state to be in! Some people arrive at this goal painstakingly, step by step, through months and weeks of self-awareness. The first time I got a glimpse of this new world beyond attachment, beyond addiction, beyond "me," it was terrifying. The urge to be free, the urge to love became a vast desert of solitude, where there was no one at my side, and at first the loneliness seemed unbearable, but that is only because we are unaccustomed to aloneness. If you manage to stay there for a while, the words will drop, the concepts will drop, and you will see. You will make contact with reality. Then you will understand what freedom is, what love is, what happiness is, what truth is, what God is, and the desert will suddenly blossom into Love. Your heart will burst into song. And it will be springtime forever.

NOTES TO MYSELF: _____

_____

_____

_____

_____

_____

_____

_____

_____

_____

_____

_____

_____

_____

CONCLUSION: NEXT STEPS

The end of all our exploring / Will be to arrive where we started /
And know the place for the first time.

—T. S. Eliot

The next step is always a return to the first step, which is awareness. Recall each day the story of the man who went to the master and asked for some wisdom that would guide him through his days, and the master answered, "Awareness, awareness, awareness." It is enough for you to simply be watchful and aware. Stop making demands on yourself, stop having expectations of yourself, stop pushing yourself, stop fixing yourself, stop trying to change other people. Simply be watchful. Make it a practice each day to ask yourself, "In whom or in what do I seek my happiness?" Then reflect on this: Whatever your answer, that's your prison. Look at it squarely. Through awareness, all that is false and neurotic within you will drop. Then you'll see transformation taking place in you, effortlessly, correctly, through the divine power of Grace.

FREE RESOURCES AT THE DE MELLO SPIRITUALITY CENTER

DeMelloCenter.com

There is an array of free resources available to you at the De Mello Spirituality Center, which is the official archive of all the works of Anthony De Mello. The Center exists to help people, just as Tony De Mello did, to realize the innate capacity to transcend stress, anxiety, and depression, and to be a light in this world—emanating from the inside out—like a beautifully lit chapel. The following resources were created to help you make your path sure and steady, and to create opportunities for you to share this journey with fellow travelers.

THE ANTHONY DE MELLO WEBSITE

The Center's website at demellospirituality.com has been designed to take you on a journey through De Mello's spirituality. The site also offers weekly blogs, an audio podcast called *The Happiness Podcast*, video excerpts from De Mello's workshops and television broadcasts, and a bookstore with all his books and full-length videos and recordings.

THE ANTHONY DE MELLO APP

You can download the Center's app to your phone and/or tablet by searching the App Store or Google Play for "DeMello Center" (no space in DeMello). You can also access the app at https://apps.apple.com/us/app/demello -center/id1466583715. It offers De Mello quotes, videos of De Mello speaking on enlightenment, the latest episode of *The Happiness Podcast*, and a meditations series on silence.

ANTHONY DE MELLO'S DAILY REMINDER EMAILS

You can sign up at the website to receive an email each day with a De Mello quote of the day and to receive notification of Center events.

ANTHONY DE MELLO ON SOCIAL MEDIA

The Center also presents De Mello's work on social media:

* Facebook at facebook.com/DeMelloSpiritualityCenter/
* Instagram at instagram.com/demellocenter/
* Twitter at twitter.com/DeMelloCenter
* YouTube at youtube.com/channel/UCF75vH8BezBDgvCfFi_EfJA

THE DE MELLO COMMUNITY PLATFORM

DeMelloCenter.com

We have also developed a virtual community platform where people can interact with each other and share ways that they are applying De Mello's approach to being happy and at peace. On this platform we will also present workshops and seminars. You can find out more about how to be part of the De Mello Community at our website.

Go to www.demellocommunity.com and click the *Join Us* button at the top right.

—**Karen Starr Venturini**,
trustee, De Mello Spirituality Center

ACKNOWLEDGMENTS

We wish to thank Penguin Random House for permission to use material from the following books:

Excerpt(s) from WELLSPRINGS: A BOOK OF SPIRITUAL EXERCISES by Anthony De Mello, copyright © 1984 by Anthony De Mello, SJ. Used by permission of Doubleday, an imprint of the Knopf Doubleday Publishing Group, a division of Penguin Random House LLC. All rights reserved.

Excerpt(s) from REDISCOVERING LIFE: AWAKEN TO REALITY by Anthony De Mello, copyright © 2012 by Center for Spiritual Exchange, Inc. Used by permission of Image Books, an imprint of Random House, a division of Penguin Random House LLC. All rights reserved.

Excerpt(s) from AWARENESS by Anthony De Mello, copyright © 1990 by The Center for Spiritual Exchange. Used by permission of Doubleday, an imprint of the Knopf Doubleday Publishing Group, a division of Penguin Random House LLC. All rights reserved.

Excerpt(s) from SADHANA: A WAY TO GOD by Anthony De Mello, SJ, copyright © 1978 by Anthony De Mello, SJ, Poona, India. Used by permission of Doubleday, an imprint of the Knopf Doubleday Publishing Group, a division of Penguin Random House LLC. All rights reserved.

Excerpt(s) from THE WAY TO LOVE: THE LAST MEDITATIONS OF ANTHONY DE MELLO by Anthony De Mello, copyright © 1991 by